"*Relationship Saboteurs* is for anyone who want[s] [to] figure out how to find and keep it. Randi Gu[nther's] [clear] and straightforward approach helps us to unde[rstand] [something] so complex: how to love and be loved."

> —Lori Gottlieb, bestselling author of *Marry Him: The Case for Settling for Mr. Good Enough*

"Once you know where the land mines are, it's much easier to avoid them. Randi Gunther's *Relationship Saboteurs* is the guidebook you need to defuse and disarm the behaviors that implode relationships."

> —Barton Goldsmith, Ph.D., psychotherapist and author of *Emotional Fitness for Couples* and *Emotional Fitness for Intimacy*

"Randi Gunther is a lifesaver. She has saved mine a few times over. With this book, she puts her decades of experience and her phenomenally deep and intuitive knowledge of couples dynamics into an easily digestable and applicable form. Whether one does the included exercises or not, a careful reading of this book will give you a roadmap to get on the path towards a healthy relationship or marriage."

> —Larry Klein, Grammy-award winning record producer, musician, and composer

relationship SABOTEURS

overcoming
the ten behaviors
that undermine
love

RANDI GUNTHER, PH.D.

New Harbinger Publications, Inc.

Publisher's Note

This publication is designed to provide accurate and authoritative information in regard to the subject matter covered. It is sold with the understanding that the publisher is not engaged in rendering psychological, financial, legal, or other professional services. If expert assistance or counseling is needed, the services of a competent professional should be sought.

Distributed in Canada by Raincoast Books

Copyright © 2010 by Randi Gunther, Ph.D.
New Harbinger Publications, Inc.
5674 Shattuck Avenue
Oakland, CA 94609
www.newharbinger.com

FSC
Mixed Sources
Product group from well-managed
forests and other controlled sources

Cert no. SW-COC-002283
www.fsc.org
© 1996 Forest Stewardship Council

Acquired by Melissa Kirk; Cover design by Amy Shoup;
Edited by Brady Kahn; Text design by Tracy Marie Carlson

Library of Congress Cataloging-in-Publication Data

Gunther, Randi.
   Relationship saboteurs : overcoming the ten behaviors that undermine love /
Randi Gunther.
      p. cm.
   ISBN 978-1-57224-746-8
   1. Interpersonal relations. 2. Social skills. 3. Personal coaching. 4. Intimacy
(Psychology) I. Title.
   HM1106.G86 2010
   646.7'7--dc22

                                                                    2010009303

12   11   10
10 9 8 7 6 5 4 3 2 1   First printing

Contents

Acknowledgments v

Prologue vii

Introduction 1

1
What Causes Relationship Sabotage? 5

2
The Process of Healing 25

3
Insecurity: "Will You Love Me Forever?" 39

4
Needing to Control: "I Run the Show" 55

5
Fear of Intimacy: "I Need You, but Not That Close" 69

6
Needing to Win: "I Dare You to Challenge Me" 85

7
Pessimism: "If You Don't Expect Anything, You
Won't Be Disappointed" 99

8
Needing to Be Center Stage: "Pay Attention to Me" 113

9
Addictions:"I've Got to Have That" 127

10
Martyrdom: "Maybe It'll Be My Turn Someday" 143

11
Defensiveness: "It's Not My Fault!" 157

12
Trust Breakers:"I Never Really Agreed to That" 169

13
Revisiting the Seven Steps to Recovery 183

14
Troubleshooting:Questions and Answers..................201

Suggested Reading 209

Acknowledgments

For my friends, colleagues, students, and patients, who, over many years, have encouraged me to write.

For Greg, my childhood sweetheart and lifelong companion, who is my most unrelenting critic and greatest champion.

For my agent, Peter Beren, a man of integrity and honor, who believed in me.

For Melissa Kirk and Jess Beebe, an enlightened team of dedicated professionals at New Harbinger, who guided me with well-placed wisdom and accurate discernment.

For my loved ones, who have patiently awaited my return from cyberspace.

Please accept my heartfelt gratitude and appreciation.

The most direct path to true intimacy is self-accountability.

Prologue

On a Saturday evening fifty-eight years ago, I accepted an offer to ice-skate with a boy. There was no way either of us could have known at that time that we would end up spending a lifetime together as lovers and best friends, or that we would be thrust together into a series of social movement that would change the face of intimate relationships forever for us and for so many others.

Throughout our life together, we have run the gamut of new-age explorations, from the challenging of role expectations and the transition from traditional male-female energy hierarchies to the egalitarian struggles couples face today. We spent years in therapy, pursued multiple individual accomplishments, and repeatedly confused our children by continuously changing our relationship's aspirations and practices.

In my mid-thirties, I returned to an education I had given up to put my husband through college and graduate school. For the next nine years, he became both mother and father to our children as I pursued four academic degrees and two licenses, often at work or in school during the day and practicing therapy anywhere people would have me in the evenings and on weekends.

It had become clear to me that being invited into the deepest realms of people's lives was a sacred rite, an incredible privilege, and a frightening responsibility. To do it well meant accumulating the best supervision, the most hours, and the opportunity to work with a wide variety of patients. In the past forty years, I have spent more than ninety thousand hours practicing a profession that continues to intrigue and gratify my passion to help individuals and couples triumph in their emotional struggles.

Because my patients have entrusted me with their innermost struggles, I have learned so much about what really drives relationships to succeed, why they crumble, and what could so easily have saved them had their participants known earlier what was wrong and what to do.

Most of us come into our relationships unprepared. New lovers typically do not search deeply enough for what may lie underneath their initial unconditional lust-love acceptance of each other. Unresolved traumatic experiences from childhood or past relationships, unconscious destructive patterns of behavior, or simply not knowing when or how to act differently—all contribute to the end of a seemingly great relationship when it might have made it had those sabotaging factors not occurred.

If people are courageous enough to explore the depths of how they learned their relationship expectations and what they need to do to bring a more aware and honest partner-self to the table, they have a much greater chance at success. New relationships can work better and troubled relationships do turn around. Most of my patients are constantly amazed at capabilities they never knew they possessed or could learn. I've lectured at conventions, supervised multiple aspiring therapists, and given dozens of workshops. At every juncture, friends, colleagues, and patients would urge me to write down what I have learned so that I could share my knowledge and experiences with more people.

Relationship Saboteurs is the beginning of that new journey for me. It has, at its core, my absolute belief that authentic change begins with self-responsibility and the courage to pursue what is right and effective, even when the people around us may not cooperate or support our efforts. Being willing to face our own limitations and work diligently to become the best people we can be, despite our legitimate sorrows, is the only path to genuine fulfillment that I know, and a prerequisite to creating successful relationships.

Introduction

Most people would think of relationship saboteurs as devious people who try to gain personal advantage at their partners' expense, practicing obviously destructive behaviors that would endanger any relationship.

This book is not about those intentional saboteurs or the pain they cause. It is about well-meaning people who, often unknowingly, practice certain subtle behaviors that undermine relationships over time.

New partners often not only accept these behaviors but also may actually be attracted by them. Yet slowly, and sometimes invisibly, these sabotaging behaviors become more intolerable. Eventually the partners of saboteurs leave the relationship, often citing reasons that have little to do with what has actually caused the relationship to end. They, themselves, do not realize that they have become allergic to a behavior that once was more acceptable.

Much of the time, relationship saboteurs are left confused, not knowing what they have done to cause their partners to pull away. Because the saboteurs don't understand what has happened, they are likely to repeat the same undermining behaviors upon entering a new relationship.

Most sabotaging behaviors are learned in childhood and reinforced by repetition. Traumatic events can be suffered throughout life, but early experiences more potently influence our subsequent relationships. People may also inherit personality characteristics and a biochemistry that make them more susceptible to holding on to negative childhood teachings. The ultimate combination of modeling, innate characteristics, and personal experience all determine whether an adult will become a relationship saboteur.

As you begin to learn more about these sabotaging behaviors, you may find them easier to recognize in your partner than in yourself. Many people do. It can be humbling to discover that you may be the one who needs to change. But if you have the courage to see what you do to sabotage your relationships, you will gain the power to transform your behavior. Every relationship you are part of, now or in the future, will benefit from what you have learned.

WHO SHOULD READ THIS BOOK

Do most of your relationships begin with the positives significantly out-weighing the negatives but over time mysteriously deteriorate? Do your partners become less tolerant of some of your behaviors that seemed fine when you first met? When your relationships end, are you frequently sur-prised or confused, unable to understand what could have gone wrong when things seemed so right?

If your answers are yes, you may be unintentionally sabotaging your rela-tionships. You could be married, divorced, habitually single, gay or straight, of either gender, or any age. Your social background or economic status makes no difference. If you are a relationship saboteur, you will unwittingly practice your subtle undermining behaviors in any important relationship. This book will help you understand where your patterns came from, what you are doing to maintain them, and how you can leave them behind.

HOW TO USE THIS BOOK

Chapter 1 describes the ten sabotaging behaviors and will help you assess your own behaviors to see if they are similar. Chapter 2 describes a seven-step recovery plan and how each step works. Each of the succeeding ten chapters covers one of the sabotaging behaviors in greater detail. As you learn more, you can determine whether you practice a particular sabotaging behavior and, if so, where it originated and how to change it. Within each of these ten chapters, you will find the seven steps to recovery and exercises to help you overcome the specific problem discussed in that chapter.

Chapter 13 will revisit the seven steps to recovery and give you some supplemental exercises you can use to overcome any of the ten sabotaging behaviors discussed in this book. You can use these same exercises to over-come other sabotaging behaviors you may have identified in your relation-ships. Chapter 14 addresses some commonly asked questions.

You can read all the chapters in sequence or skip to the chapters that seem most relevant to you. I recommend reading chapters 1 and 2 even if you choose to skip others. You will find the exercises in this book valuable, whether you are in a new relationship, in between partners, or in a long-term commitment. You can practice them alone or with a partner. The exercises work equally well for men and women, and regardless or whether you are with someone of the same or opposite sex.

You will want to keep a detailed journal as you work through the exercises. Being able to refer back to your journal through the coming months will help you understand more clearly how your behavior patterns have developed and how to hold on to the new vision of who you want to become.

The exercises are deeply personal. Whether you do them alone or with a partner is up to you, but if you do choose a partner, make sure the person you include will be able to help rather than hinder you in your recovery. Partners, friends, professionals, and self-help groups can be wonderful supports if they encourage you to keep your focus. They can also be unhelpful indulgers if they have their own investment in keeping you the way you were.

SOME WORDS OF ENCOURAGEMENT

I have used this book's seven-step recovery plan with many individuals and couples. The rate of success is very high. Not only have they been able to change their behaviors and create more fulfilling relationships, but they have also found a new kind of self-respect and pride in their accomplishments. The skills they've learned have helped them become more effective in every kind of relationship. Facing their own accountability for what they may have done to harm their relationships has helped them discover a deeper appreciation for the positives they have to offer.

You can develop your own course of action and significantly change your behavior and your relationships, or you can call on professional help to speed your process along. Deeply entrenched patterns are often difficult to see and correct on your own. You will always be the most reliable expert on yourself, but other trusted opinions can help you stay on track.

1

What Causes Relationship Sabotage?

Relationships are formed from the first moment of our lives. The way we are touched, the approving or rejecting voices we hear, and the interactions we observe all become part of the positive and negative alchemy that makes each of us the unique person we are destined to become.

Our emotional and physical interactions with our childhood caretakers form the core of what we will expect in our adult relationships. Children are small, powerless people whose world comes to them prepackaged. They do not know whether their own experience is better or worse than it should be. They can only maneuver their way through a maze of approval and disapproval, and struggle to ensure that they will at least survive.

WHERE DO SABOTAGING PATTERNS BEGIN?

Sabotaging patterns can be learned at any time in life, but the earlier they are observed or experienced, the greater the chance they will be unconsciously internalized. When negative childhood patterns emerge in adult relationships, it may be difficult to discern where and how they originated, reconstructing them is like putting together a three-dimensional puzzle with pieces missing, but they hold the information we need to understand the present.

Childhood Interaction

If children are fortunate, they are exposed to successful relationships as they mature. They also receive accurate and supportive feedback on how their own personality traits might aid or hinder their relationships with family members. Sadly, many parents are unable to demonstrate successful relationship behaviors because they themselves have never learned these behaviors.

Ideally, throughout each developmental stage of life, people have opportunities to alter negative childhood patterns they may have developed. If they are not hindered by internalized limitations, they can seek more information and learn from the successes and failures of each new interaction. With each new opportunity, they can continually better the balance between satisfaction and sorrow.

Inherited Dysfunction

Family patterns are transferred from generation to generation. Unless questioned, they will become traditions, passed on exactly as they were learned.

Unfortunately, children cannot sort out dysfunctional interactions from those that are not dysfunctional. They experience both positive and negative interactions as an expected part of family life, and assume they are necessary components of every succeeding relationship. If their parents don't learn from their own mistakes while their children are young, they will pass on those dysfunctional patterns.

When those children become adults, they will likely create relationships that are similar to those they witnessed and experienced in childhood. Familiarity is a powerful magnet. It will draw people to re-create what they were taught, even if those lessons were unfulfilling or painful. Their partners will also come with their own set of healthy or damaged relationship expectations. Given the sheer possibility of crisscrossing positive and negative connections, it's no wonder so many hopeful relationships stumble and fall over time.

IT'S NOT ME, IT'S YOU—OR IS IT?

Whether from childhood teachings or societal reinforcement, most people believe their relationships fail because they didn't choose the right partner or because they should have done something differently. It's easy to fall into rationalizing traps that encourage you to look for accountability outside of yourself. It feels better to believe these kinds of statements:

- "My partner just isn't there for me."

- "No matter what I do or say, he won't bend."

- "All you have to do is make one big mistake, and she's gone."

- "He's so self-centered, he'll never understand me."

Or you may rationalize with these kinds of assumptions:

- "I just can't find anyone decent, so I start off compromising. Why do I even think I have a chance?"

- "No one makes it long-term anymore."

- "Men are commitment phobic, and women only stay with guys who can take good care of them."

But what if *you* are the problem? What if you have had a series of relationships that ended before you wanted them to? Or what if you're in a long-term committed relationship that has become contaminated and you don't know what when wrong?

ARE YOU SABOTAGING YOUR OWN RELATIONSHIPS?

If you are someone who has started relationships determined to love and be loved, given everything you had to make the relationships work, yet watched them slowly fall apart no matter how hard you tried, your own behaviors may be the reason.

It's not easy for anyone to look at that possibility. New partners often refrain from telling you what they don't like, hoping your good qualities will outweigh your liabilities if they just hang on long enough. Established partners may feel cumulative resentments but either have not shared them or have resigned themselves to accepting those behaviors because you've been unwilling or unable to change them.

Whatever the case, sabotaging behaviors slowly build toxicity in a partnership that might otherwise have succeeded. What once may have been tolerable or even acceptable eventually evokes an emotionally allergic reaction in the partner of a saboteur.

It takes courage for any of us to turn the mirror of responsibility on ourselves. It's less painful to rationalize our own negative reactions as being justified by what others have done to us. But when your hopeful relationships always end in the same way, or your long-term relationships continue to falter, you are probably the one who has to change.

Most relationship saboteurs are not intentionally destructive. They don't set out to torment their partners or to destroy their relationships. In fact, most of the people I've worked with who have repeatedly failed in their relationships are heartsick about it, and don't understand why their relationships haven't worked out.

Some committed relationships do manage to survive despite long-term sabotaging interactions. The partners in a continual conflict-love relationship may be unwilling to give up what they treasure about each other, despite the cost. Their relationship continues to endure, but it will always operate on less than its full potential unless the partners stop their sabotaging behaviors.

Sabotaging behaviors can take many forms, but they share some common characteristics:

- They often are tolerable, even desirable to some partners at the beginning of a relationship.

- They are not meant to create the damage or disruption that they do.

- Their negative influence on a relationship evolves over time.

- They are often subtly hidden and may be expressed as a different problem in the relationship.

- They may be more tolerable when a relationship is new but will eventually destroy its ability to regenerate.

- If these behaviors are challenged, the partner doing them will usually feel righteous and offended when confronted.

The following exercise will help you determine whether or not you have sabotaged your past relationships. You may want to take notes or write your answers in a separate notebook or journal.

EXERCISE: Have You Been a Relationship Saboteur?

To determine if you practice relationship sabotage, rate your answers to the following questions on a scale of 1 to 5, in which 1 = never, 2 = sometimes, 3 = usually, 4 = often, and 5 = always.

1. If you queried all your significant partners, would their complaints be similar?

2. Have you dismissed your partners' requests for change as unimportant?

3. Do you continue with certain patterns of behavior, even when they are clearly driving your partner away?

4. When your partners have been distressed with you, have you responded defensively and justified what you're doing?

5. Did anyone in your childhood justify hurtful behaviors that happened to you or others?

6. Would you be unable to tolerate a partner behaving the way you behave in your relationships?

7. When you start to see your relationships crumble, do you lean even more heavily on certain patterns of behavior that have not worked in the past?

8. When you're confronted with behaviors your partner doesn't like, do you try to reverse the blame and focus on your partner's faults instead?

9. Do you expect your partner to excuse your faults because you have other good qualities?

10. Are you likely to blame your partner for behaviors you are employing?

11. When your relationships have ended, have you usually felt self-righteous and that you are not the one who should be blamed?

12. Do you believe the reason your relationships fail is that you just haven't found the right person?

Now add up your total score. If the total is 1 to 24, you are more than likely not a relationship saboteur. You may do some distancing in your relationships when you are off-kilter, but your partner should not use that as a reason to disconnect from the relationship. If your score is between 25 and 36, you could be eroding the trust of your partner and should begin your recovery work, so you can move in a more positive direction. If your score is over 36, you could already be sabotaging your relationships and need to commit yourself to a new way of being.

TEN COMMON RELATIONSHIP-SABOTAGING BEHAVIORS

The ten most common relationship-sabotaging behaviors may not be obvious or even offensive when a relationship is new. Most new partners, bathed in the wonder of romantic lust, do not see these behaviors as serious issues. Over time, however, they slowly dissolve intimacy. When the damage is done, the relationship may be beyond repair.

The following sections will give you a snapshot of what these behavior patterns look like. Each of these behaviors will be explored in detail in later chapters.

Insecurity: "Will You Love Me Forever?"

Anxiety, possessiveness, and jealousy are the constant companions of people who suffer from insecurity in their relationships. Fear of anticipated loss, whether substantiated or not, interferes with their ability to fully experience the positive aspects of their relationships.

New partners of anxious people may initially be attracted to their vulnerability and need for reassurance. Rescuers, particularly, may feel more important in a new relationship with someone who is anxious, and take pleasure in providing whatever is asked. They feel rewarded when their insecure partners feel safe in their presence.

Unfortunately, people who are innately insecure cannot be soothed out of their continuous distress. Over time, their partners begin to feel invalidated and ineffective when they are unable to stop the endless need for reassurance, and they may eventually transfer their devotion to others who are easier to help.

. ARE YOU TOO INSECURE IN YOUR RELATIONSHIPS?

By answering the following questions, you can recognize whether insecurity has been a factor in your relationships:

- Are you likely to focus more on whether your relationship will last than on enjoying it as it happens?

- Do you find yourself obsessing on the slightest change in your partner that might signal a decrease in interest?

- Are you threatened by your partner's other close relationships?

- Do you find yourself often seeking reassurance?

- Do you constantly worry that your partner may leave you?

If the answers to these questions are yes, you may have sabotaged your relationships because you were too insecure. Chapter 3 will help you understand your behavior and provide the steps to overcome this problem.

Needing to Control: "I Run the Show"

People who have a compulsive need to control others believe that they are not only entitled but also obligated to do so. They are not comfortable unless they are micromanaging their partner's life, and sincerely believe that they are the only ones who can do things correctly.

This need to dominate may hide an underlying fear of being controlled. Controlling people may have been raised by similarly overbearing parents who forced them into obedient subservience. As a result, they may be determined never to be in that role again. Or the opposite can be true: the controller may have been allowed to rule the roost as a self-appointed child dictator and have no intention of giving up those rights in an adult relationship.

Initially, controlling partners may appear to be expert caretakers, anticipating their partner's every need. They are so willing to take care of every aspect of the relationship that they seduce their new partner into self-indulgent comfort. But over time, the price becomes evident; all decisions about the relationship are made unilaterally and delivered without options.

Controlling people are easier to take when they wield their power with compassion and fairness. They're harder to tolerate when their decisions are based on biases that cannot be challenged or changed. At the beginning of a relationship, they are usually careful to rule with tact and diplomacy. Once their dominance is established, though, they can revert to dictatorship and may be difficult to unseat.

DO YOU NEED TO CONTROL YOUR RELATIONSHIP?

By answering the following questions, you can determine if needing to control has been a factor in your relationships:

- Do you only feel comfortable when you make the rules?

- Are you resentful if your partner argues with your decisions?

- Have past partners complained that you dominated the relationship?

- Are you ever able to let your partner tell you what to do?

- If there is a conflict over a direction in the relationship, do you insist on having your way?

- If your partner doesn't do what you want, do you punish him or her?

Learning to share decision making is crucial for a relationship to work. Chapter 4 addresses the need to control and how to overcome this problem.

Fear of Intimacy: "I Need You, but Not That Close"

Everyone has some fear of too much physical or emotional closeness because all intimate connections require surrendering some personal independence. Most people manage those fears by entering relationships gradually and leaving exit room if necessary. If the balance between closeness and autonomy works for both partners, they will continue exploring an ever-deepening connection. If they cannot sustain that mutual comfort, they will eventually drift apart.

People with deeper fears of intimacy may be torn between desire and expectation of disaster. They cannot differentiate between a deepening commitment and entrapment. That internal conflict drives them to alternately seek and reject closeness with their partners.

As their relationships deepen, the terror of losing themselves to their partner's needs intensifies, and they bolt, temporarily or permanently. They are often labeled "commitment phobic," partners who can only love with one foot out the door.

DO YOU FEAR BEING TRAPPED IN INTIMATE OBLIGATIONS?

By answering the following questions, you can determine if fear of intimacy is a factor in your relationships:

- Are you only able to be open and passionate when you're in control?

- Do you find yourself retreating from your relationships when they seem too close?

- Have you become an expert in convincing your partner to reenter the relationship after he or she has given up on you?

- Do you feel sincere in your desire to connect, but later become surprised when you feel trapped?

- Do your partners tell you they don't trust your love anymore?

Chapter 5 addresses fear of intimacy and how to overcome this problem.

Needing to Win: "I Dare You to Challenge Me"

Verbal competition in relationships can be fun. The excitement of winning a disagreement or driving a point home can enhance the passion of a relationship. Partners can use those interactions to gain a better understanding of each other's point of view—that is, if both are into the game. But if either partner needs to bow out of the competition and the other needs to keep winning, the result may be destructive.

Once they are in a competitive interaction, people who have to win have great difficulty backing down, no matter what's at stake. They are usually poor losers, turning from friend to foe very quickly if their opinions don't triumph. Activated by their compulsion to make the final point, they continue arguing until their partners are down for the count.

Once the battle is over, they often act as if nothing were wrong, and are offended if their partners aren't interested in reconnecting. "It was just an disagreement," they contend. "What's the big deal?"

Compulsive winners tend to look for partners who are willing opponents or those who give in quickly. Their partners have only three choices: fight, accept defeat, or leave the battlefield.

DO YOU CHOOSE WINNING OVER CARING?

By answering the following questions, you can determine if needing to win has been a factor in your relationships:

- When your partner gets the upper hand, are you able to make a gracious retreat, or must you have the final say?

- To what extent will you go to prove that you're right and your partner is wrong?

- Will you risk intimacy just to win a point?

- When you're challenged, are you quick to assume a fighting stance?

- Are you a sore loser?

- Is it easy for you to be close again after the battle is over?

The scars of needless battles will eventually destroy the love in any relationship. Chapter 6 addresses the need to win and how to overcome this problem.

Pessimism: "If You Don't Expect Anything, You Won't Be Disappointed"

Children are not born pessimistic. They have to learn it from adults. Some families must struggle to meet their basic needs or have suffered multiple losses. They can understandably adopt an attitude that any expectation of positives will bring only more disappointment.

Others believe that pessimism is honorable, the way to face reality without being foolish. Some may even see optimism as superstitious, certain to deliver the opposite if you are seduced into believing in a better outcome. There are also, sadly, highly dysfunctional families who express their own despair by destroying dreams, even if they could come true.

If children born into pessimistic families also have inherited depression, they have a double burden. The combination of a negative childhood environment and a depressive biochemistry is a significant weight to bear.

Mistrust and pessimism are magnets for optimistic people who thrive on bringing joy into darkness. Winnie-the-Pooh and his eternally sad friend Eeyore are a great example of this kind of duo. But even tenacious cheerleaders can't stick around forever when their partners won't believe in a more hopeful future.

ARE YOU UNABLE TO TRUST IN GOOD OUTCOMES?

By answering the following questions, you can determine if being a pessimist has been a factor in your relationships:

- Do you often invalidate your partner's devotion because you don't think it will last?

- Have past partners complained that nothing they do makes you believe they care about you?

- Do you reject hopeful outcomes as if they could never happen to you?

- Does too much happiness make you uncomfortable?

- Do you seem to attract partners who are consistently more hopeful than you?

A continued attachment to pessimism will eventually defeat the most optimistic of partners. Chapter 7 addresses pessimism and how to overcome this problem.

Needing to Be Center Stage: "Pay Attention to Me"

People who need to be center stage inappropriately draw attention to themselves. Whether in a group of people or in a personal relationship, they often miss the social cues that tell them when others are overloaded, and they show little interest in others' opinions or feelings.

Childhood neglect or overindulgence can be an explanation for how people become this way. But such experience doesn't always predict this behavior. Some people just can't seem to stay involved in a conversation unless they are the main topic of discussion. They may not intend to be inappropriately demanding, but they can't seem to stop their desire for a one-way interaction. Their partners may have difficulty getting a word in edgewise. Center-stage personalities are superb at turning every conversation back to themselves.

ARE YOU A CENTER-STAGE PERSONALITY?

By answering the following questions, you can determine if needing to be center stage has been a factor in your past relationships:

- Do you get bored when people divert their attention away from you?

- Is it hard for you to get interested in someone else's conversation unless it pertains to you?

- Do you find yourself verbally monopolizing situations?

- Do you feel neglected when your partner doesn't put you first?

- Do you have tantrums or withdraw if you can't have your way?

Do you want to have an audience or an interested lover? Chapter 8 addresses the need to be center stage and how to overcome this problem.

Addictions: "I've Got to Have That"

Addictions are competitive lovers. They are self-destructive seductions masquerading as desirable behaviors, and they lull people away from the values and behaviors that keep relationships viable. If addictions are extreme and show up at the beginning of a relationship, those partners who understand their power shy away, knowing that there is little they can do to compete.

Unfortunately, there are some addictive behaviors that seem both acceptable and exciting when love is new. The passion of addictive cravings may be turned toward a new partner, adding intensity to the relationship. Then, as time goes by, that same passion will eventually be redirected toward other desires, and the resulting abandonment becomes intolerable to the addict's partner. Addicts become relationship saboteurs, slowly withdrawing the focused love that attracted their partners at the beginning of the relationship and transferring it to their new focus.

Addictions are intense cravings that often cause their users to do things they later deeply regret. You can be addicted not only to substances but also to relationships, materialistic acquisitions, or even ideologies. Addictions can drive anyone to put aside other values, obligations, or commitments, in pursuit of a journey that too often ends in irrevocable loss.

ARE YOU AN ADDICT?

By answering the following questions, you can determine if addictions have been a factor in your relationships:

- Do you hide your behavior when your cravings erupt?

- Are you likely to get defensive when your partner holds you accountable for your choices?

- Do you give in to desires that keep you from being the person you want to be?

- Do your relationships fall apart because of your addictive behavior?

- Are your behaviors self-destructive?

- Are you unable to stop your relationship-destructive behaviors even when you know you risk losing your partner?

- Do you cause others heartbreak but feel unable to stop?

Love cannot flourish in a triangle. Chapter 9 addresses addictive behavior and offers seven steps to overcome this problem.

Martyrdom: "Maybe It'll Be My Turn Someday"

Being with a martyr is like having a credit card you can never pay off. The martyr's attempt to build reciprocal obligation is one of the saddest and most ineffective ways to manipulate. People who encourage their partners to take advantage of their generosity and then suffer in silence cannot maintain this imbalance forever. Their partners will eventually get a detailed report of how much they've been given and what they need to do to make amends.

Martyrs fear that they can never do enough to ensure the reciprocity they may need in the future. Yet they continue to adapt and accommodate to their partner's every need, hoping that someday they will get their reward.

People who become martyrs have usually been taken advantage of as children. Whether their caretakers were abusive, neglectful, or manipulative with guilt or threats of abandonment, they often grow to be adults who come into relationships predefeated. They are self-inflicting victims, giving away personal power as an emotional dowry.

People who partner up with martyrs may be initially attracted to what seems like selfless generosity. They may even initially bask in the sacrifices that masquerade as unconditional love and acceptance. Unfortunately, the bill eventually will come due. If the debt is too high, leaving the relationship may be the only option available to the martyr's partner.

ARE YOU A MARTYR IN YOUR RELATIONSHIPS?

By answering the following questions, you can determine if martyrdom has been a factor in your relationships:

- Do you feel used and unfairly discarded when your relationships end?

- Is it hard for you to ask your partners for what you feel you deserve?

- Are you proud of yourself for asking so little in a relationship?

- Do you consistently attract selfish or self-centered partners?

- Do you wonder if you'll ever get taken care of by anyone?

People rarely expect to pay more for the benefits of a relationship than they do up front. Chapter 10 addresses the problem of martyrdom.

Defensiveness: "It's Not My Fault!"

When partners are defending themselves against a perceived emotional attack, they cannot listen, learn, or change. They are driven to invalidate what they feel as a critical challenge.

If you're like most people, you will react defensively when you feel threatened. It's difficult to look into the eyes of someone who matters and accept unasked-for criticism without trying to justify what you've done, especially if the accusations don't feel fair. Most people are unsettled when this happens, but they try to consider the source and the situation before they react. Chronic defenders do not have that luxury. If they believe that an accusation is focused in their direction, they cannot respond with anything but a justification for their behavior.

Chronic defenders may respond to an assumed attack in several ways, but each has the same intent, to get out from under the accusation by invalidating it:

Reversing the blame: "What about you? You do that, too."

Insulting the other person's intelligence: "That's a really stupid thing to say."

Making an excuse: "You're being so unfair. You know how much I had to do today."

Exaggerating dramatically: "Why don't you just tell me I'm completely worthless and get it over with?"

Citing one exception to the accusation: "I don't always forget to call you. I did a couple of months ago."

Arguing by picking apart each point and countering it: "That's totally untrue. You don't have your facts right."

Withdrawing: "This is so ridiculous, I'm not even going to talk to you about it."

If you respond this way, your partner usually will try to invalidate your invalidating response, which leads to a downward spiral. The cycle of attack and defense increases. After several rounds, no one will be listening anymore and nothing will be solved.

Defenders often attract partners who are critical and controlling. The dance of accusation and defense becomes chronic bickering that's often witnessed by others. It will go on until one partner gives up and either sacrifices himself or herself to the relationship or gets out to survive.

ARE YOU A CHRONIC DEFENDER?

By answering the following questions, you can determine if defensiveness has been a factor in your relationships:

- When your partner finds fault with something you've done, is your first response to challenge the accusation?

- Are you ever able to listen to a complaint without invalidating what your partner is telling you?

- Are you open to seeing yourself through your partner's eyes, even if it feels critical?

- Is there any way your partner can approach you with a grievance without your defending your actions?

You can learn how to listen to your partner's complaints without feeling that you must agree with his or her point of view. Chapter 11 addresses defensiveness and how to overcome this problem.

Trust Breakers: "I Never Really Agreed to That"

Betrayal is the worst of all relationship-sabotaging behaviors. People who make a practice of breaking promises, rewriting history, ignoring agreements, or denying their partner's reality break hearts and destroy faith.

Of course, many of the agreements lovers make at the beginning of relationships have to be renegotiated as time goes by. People change and relationships mature. But partners who live in each other's hearts are committed to sharing who they are and what they do as their relationships evolve. Both agree that there are no reasons valid enough to keep anything secret that could adversely affect either partner. They have total faith in the sacredness of that agreement.

Trust is faith that what is promised will come true or that the reasons it can't will be explained. For children, trust is the foundation of the ability to love and to feel safe. If they are consistently faced with disappointment or disillusionment, they come to believe that what is promised is not real and cannot be counted upon. The earlier those negative experiences happen, the more likely those children will grow into adults who can neither trust nor be trusted.

When adult trust breakers are busted, they will do whatever is necessary to get out of being held accountable. If their partners feel too uncertain to hold their ground, they may be susceptible to the trust breaker's ability to get them to believe again.

Many partners continue to love their trust breakers even though they know that more betrayals lie ahead. Attachments don't always make sense, and enough love can rationalize the most painful of outcomes. But, if the couple stays together, the cycles of belief and disillusionment will take their toll. Trust is the foundation of everything that matters. When it's gone, all agreements become invalid.

ARE YOU A TRUST BREAKER?

By answering the following questions, you can determine if being a trust breaker has been a factor in your past relationships:

- Do you blame your partner when you are clearly responsible for a relationship problem?

- Do you keep your partner from knowing information that would cost you options were he or she to know?

- Do you consistently choose to do things that betray your partner's trust?

- Are you willing to take advantage of your partner's gullibility by telling him or her things that aren't true?

- Would you stay in a relationship with someone who behaves like you?

Whether by omission or commission, lies will eventually create a web of destruction that no relationship can survive. Chapter 12 addresses being a trust breaker and how to overcome this problem.

WHY SABOTEURS MAY INITIALLY ATTRACT THEIR PARTNERS

It may seem odd that these potentially destructive behaviors take so long to evolve as sabotaging influences. Not only are they much less noticeable in the early stages of a relationship, but, as mentioned previously, these behaviors may actually be initially attractive to certain partners. When they cease to be desirable, the unsuspecting relationship saboteur often cannot understand why what once was acceptable has now become a liability.

If you have identified yourself as a relationship saboteur, it's important to recognize how a new lover who finds your behavior initially desirable can grow to resent it over time. If you understand the process, you may be able to minimize or eradicate the negative effects when your sabotaging behavior begins to cause problems.

Here are the initially attractive sides of the ten relationship saboteurs:

Insecurity. Insecure people genuinely appreciate being comforted and often attract others who enjoy being needed.

Needing to control. Controlling people can pay exquisite attention to their partners.

Fear of intimacy. Those who avoid intimacy may be enticing because they are always a little out of reach.

Needing to win. Competitive people are challenging and can be fun to interact with.

Pessimism. Negative people attract people who love to help.

Needing to be center stage. A center-stage person can allow tentative people the time they need to get more comfortable before they interact.

Addictions. People with addictive personalities make their new lovers feel exciting and desirable.

Martyrdom. Martyred victims make their new partners feel treasured by anticipating their every need.

Defensiveness. Defensive people are attractive to people who like to escalate arguments.

Trust breakers. Trust breakers attract people who expect to be disappointed but still hope to find the one person who won't betray them.

You may find yourself in more than one of these sabotaging behaviors or have been attracted to partners who practice them. Some of these behaviors overlap in their symptoms or cover deeper problems that may lie beneath.

In later chapters, you will be better able to identify your own patterns and those of the people you have loved or might love in the future. Despite the capacity of these behaviors to destroy the intimacy in any relationship, every one of these sabotaging behaviors can be healed. It takes courage to look honestly at who you are, but your willingness to leave sabotaging behaviors behind will bring you greater confidence and success in every relationship you pursue.

2

The Process of Healing

It's not easy to change behavior that you have been practicing for a long time. Transformation requires that you leave your past behind without the comfort of knowing what your future will be. You will feel more confident in taking that leap if you can trust in a healing plan that makes sense.

THE SEVEN-STEP PLAN

The seven steps to healing introduced in this chapter will give you an overview of the changes you must make to take you from where you are to where you want to be. The following chapters will show you how to use these steps more specifically, to overcome the ten most common relationship-sabotaging behaviors. The steps may seem a little overwhelming at first, but small successes will happen as soon as you begin, and those improvements will keep you from being discouraged along the way.

Step One: Observing Your Behavior Without Judgment

To learn more about what you have done to sabotage your relationships, you need to observe your behavior without succumbing to self-criticism, or negative self-talk. Negative self-talk is a repeat of critical parental remarks that you internalized as a child. Without realizing it, you may continue to make those critical statements to yourself whenever you feel bad about something you've done:

- "What an idiot you are."

- "You keep doing things that screw up your life."

- "Why can't you learn?"

- "No one will ever like you if you act like this."

- "You knew what you were doing was wrong. Why didn't you stop?"

Talking to yourself in this way when you have done something you regret is counterproductive. It's too hard to remember to behave differently when you're trying to defend yourself against a disdainful inner authority. If you are courageous enough to look at your negative behavior, you must give yourself the support you need to work on changing it. Self-criticism will only slow down your process of healing.

If you listen carefully to your own internal dialogue, you will likely hear the way a parent disciplined you when you were young. If a parent responded to your mistakes with disappointment, anger, impatience, or shame, you may find yourself repeating these comments in your own head as an adult.

To change your negative behavior, you must eliminate those destructive inner dialogues. When you recognize actions that have hurt your relationships in the past, simply observe them without allowing any inner judgments. You will expedite the process of healing if you look objectively at your negative relationship behavior without putting yourself down.

GETTING HELP ALONG THE WAY

If you are currently in a relationship and still have your partner's love and confidence, it will immediately help the relationship to tell your partner that you are aware of what you are doing and determined to change it. Just saying that can help you get the time and support you'll need to change.

If you feel embarrassed or want to judge yourself harshly, let those judgments go. If you feel the urge to deny or rationalize what you are doing, try to stop. This is the time to collect as much information as you can without allowing anything to cloud your ability to learn.

If you are not presently in a relationship, think about those partnerships that were significant to you and observe them as if they were happening now. Remember: do not let your self-evaluation devolve into embarrassment or shame.

Answering the following questions may help:

- What have you done that consistently offended, hurt, or pushed your partner away?

- What results were you looking for when you acted that way?

- What usually happened instead of what you wanted?

- Do you wish things had worked out differently? If so, how?

- What were you feeling when you repeated behavior that you know has not worked in the past?

- What did you do to try to make things better?

- Can you observe these past interactions without blaming your partners or yourself?

Step Two: Finding the Taproots of Your Behavior

Once you have objectively observed and identified your relationship-sabotaging behavior, you will be ready to explore its origins. Start by following your current behaviors back into the past. Think of this as a journey down the taproot of a tree, to its deepest core. By following this taproot, you will be able to see how your life experiences have created and reinforced this negative behavior.

Your relationship behavior patterns have developed from your inherited personality characteristics, the relationships you've observed, and your own experiences. To find the taproots of your sabotaging behavior, you will need to remember any traumatic interactions that may hold the seeds of your current behavior.

REPEATED IRRATIONAL BEHAVIORS

People are unlikely to repeat behavior that doesn't work unless it's driven by unquestioned conscious or unconscious childhood teachings. If, for instance, you were told as a child that a certain consequence would result if you did something, but that prediction never came true, you would be less likely to believe it would happen the next time.

But if the caretakers you were dependent on insisted that you continue to believe in that improbability, you may have accepted that their reasoning was sounder than yours. To challenge your caretakers might have risked their approval, a choice too difficult for most children to make. If children continue to accept their caretakers' irrational statements, it may limit their ability to believe their own experiences later on.

The personality of each child will help or hinder whatever damage may result from these crazy-making interpretations. Some children come into this world happy, resilient, and outgoing. When the disappointment of a broken promise happens, they can shrug it off and start over with renewed hope. Others are not as fortunate. They may be born more anxious or less able to tolerate frustration. When their expectations are consistently under-mined, they may hold on more dearly to unlikely futures or be unable to believe any longer that promises will come true.

A combination of factors produces each unique human being. This personal mix of genetics, modeling, and parental teachings is then modified by every experience that follows. From these components, we develop the roles we expect to play in relationships and what we expect from our partners. If we don't challenge the old teachings, our past will define our future.

Asking the following questions may help you locate the taproots of your sabotaging behavior:

- Which parts of your negative behavior did you learn and which seem more innate to your personality?

- Was your environment helpful or hostile to your development?

- What were your caretakers' expectations of you?

- What kind of relationships did you observe around you?

- Were there any past traumas that could be affecting you now?

- What were the important ways you were nurtured or invalidated?

- When did you first begin acting in these negative ways in relationships?

Step Three: Identifying the Triggers

The next step is to determine what sets off your sabotaging behavior. Emotional or physical triggers—in the form of a simple phrase, a tone of voice, a gesture, or a facial expression—can remind you of a childhood event and bring the past into the present, whether or not you are conscious of what you may be responding to. Even environments that remind you of past traumatic events can affect what's happening in your relationship.

Triggers are established in childhood. They are reinforced throughout your life every time a negative sequence is repeated. Familiarity is a powerful mask, and you may not even recognize when your old behavior is being triggered. An unconscious memory may set off negative behavior in your present relationship before you realize that you could have had a better response.

RECOGNIZING TRIGGERS

Sometimes it's a combination of events that leads to a negative reaction. These triggers may be obvious or subtle and harder to identify. If you observe yourself sabotaging your relationship, you will want to retrace your steps and try to remember what happened before you began reacting negatively. You may have to go back hours or days to discover when the sequence of events began that eventually led to your negative response.

Once you understand the sequence of events, you can try to recall when you first felt that way in your life. See if the present situation feels similar to what you experienced back then. Remember where you were, who was present, and how you felt at the time. The more details, the more helpful the memory will be.

You will want to ask yourself these questions: In what ways are the past and present situations similar? Does the relationship with your current partner feel similar to one from your past? (Note: The earlier the relationship, the more potent its effect may be.) It will help if you write your observations in your journal for later reference after you've had a chance to work with what you've discovered.

The most important clue to knowing you are being triggered is the intensity and quality of emotion you feel in the moment. Intense feelings that may seem too strong for the situation at hand are often associated with traumatic childhood experiences. Listen deeply to those feelings and see if they will help you to rediscover the memories you need.

The goal is to get a closer look at where your behaviors began. Once you identify the childhood experience that triggers your current feelings, you can anticipate your responses. That will give you time to choose an alternative reaction. The earlier you can recognize a trigger pattern, the more chance you will have to replace self-destructive behaviors with effective ones.

If you find yourself being triggered into negative behavior, these questions will help:

- When have you felt this way before?

- What was happening to you then?

- What did you feel?

- What was expected of you?

- What was the outcome?

- How is the present situation similar?

- What seems to be the present trigger that activated your reaction?

Step Four: Examining When You Are Most Susceptible

Life's trials can vary dramatically. When things are going well, we have more resilience, more time to think of options, and more reserves. A trigger that can set off a cascade of negative behavior when we're tired, pressured, or frightened may not provoke us when we're on an even keel. The same sequence of events that could throw you over the edge at one time might only evoke a gentle irritation at another. Learning to recognize when you are the most susceptible to reacting negatively gives you more leverage in maintaining your promises to yourself and to the one you love.

Perhaps you have unconsciously chosen a partner who reminds you of someone from your past. If your emotional reaction to your partner is similar to what you experienced before, you may automatically behave just as you did back then. Or your behavior may be triggered only when someone else threatens to take away your partner and activates a jealousy triangle you had as a child. You may be more susceptible to your triggers in a certain location or while experiencing a specific type of weather, hearing a familiar piece of music, or viewing a scene in a movie or TV program. Don't be surprised if the reasons seem trivial at the time. They are often clues to much deeper issues that lie underneath.

WHAT CAUSES TRIGGERS TO ACTIVATE?

Some people are naturally more susceptible than others to triggers. Your inborn nature can make you more susceptible as well. Sensitive people are more reactive to all stimuli. Naturally resilient people don't react as strongly even when they're under stress.

Whatever your basic nature, your present state can exaggerate or calm your trigger reactions. For example, if you are facing multiple losses or demands, your adrenaline may be running higher than usual and you may be reactive to a situation that would normally not push in so hard. Depression and stress may also be factors. Whenever you feel "close to breaking" or that you "just can't handle one more thing," you may find yourself with a low tolerance for disappointment or challenge.

Once you understand when you are the most susceptible, you can compensate. Knowing when your reserves are down and your needs are high can make the difference between succeeding and failing.

SLOWING DOWN YOUR REACTIVITY

Asking these questions may help you slow down your reactivity:

- What's typically going on in your life when you seem more reactive to your triggers?

- Does your partner remind you of anyone from your childhood?

- If so, how?

- Which of your personality traits drives your reactivity?

- Do trigger situations feel familiar? If so, how?

- Is there anything your partner could do to change your response?

- How old do you feel when you react to a trigger?

Step Five: Seeking a New Vision and Finding Alternative Behavior

Steps one through four will help you determine which behaviors you want to change, trace the origins of these behaviors, and understand your vulnerabilities. These steps will form the foundation for your transformation. Steps five through seven will help you determine the person you want to become and to make certain you meet, and hold on to, your goal.

Changing an instilled set of reactions can be difficult, for the combination of your inherited nature and life experiences provides a powerful drag chute. Many people are so used to failing in relationships that they have accepted their situations as unavoidable. You need to define an alternative path, so that the one you've been on no longer feels like your only choice.

THREE CRUCIAL COMMITMENTS

Change can begin when you make the commitment to do the following three things:

1. Identify what you are leaving behind.

2. Have a vision of who you want to become.

3. Decide how you can make it happen and ensure that your new behavior will hold.

It's always easier to leave the past behind when you are excited about the future. Even so, it's sometimes hard to stay on course when the comfort of old behavior beckons. To avoid feeling discouraged, you will need to keep your eye on where you are headed. The exercises in subsequent chapters will help you focus on your specific sabotaging behaviors, but here are some general guidelines.

You will want to begin your journey by finding new people to emulate, those who react successfully when they are confronted with relationship challenges. Observing these new role models, you will be able to consistently compare your past negative behavior to more successful behavior.

The past will continue to insert itself as you try to change your responses. If you find yourself repeatedly slipping back, you may find it helpful to go back in time and imagine the kind of caretaker you would have wanted as a child, rather than the one who taught you sabotaging behavior. Some people effectively use this new internalized parent as their role model. A willing and helpful partner can also be an asset, as can a professional who may be able to assist you in separating your past responses from those you want to develop.

As you do the exercises in each chapter, you will begin to formulate your own personal set of goals and how to realize them. What's important to remember is that you are emerging from deeply set patterns into a world you do not yet know.

THE FOURTH COMMITMENT

Once you have your vision in place, you must commit to exerting self-discipline and patience. Holding on to new behavior takes practice when old habit patterns are strong, especially if they were learned through traumatic experiences. The emotional grooves of dysfunctional behavior are deep and easily repeated. The new path is uncertain. You must stay conscious at every crossroads and choose the direction that takes you where you want to go.

For each of the ten destructive relationship behaviors explored in this book, there are better alternatives. Even if you are currently in an established relationship, you will see positive changes from the moment you begin your journey.

SOME GUIDING QUESTIONS

You may want to write the answers to the following questions in your journal. Then keep your journal in a spot where you can ask yourself these questions every day and compare your answers:

1. What behaviors are you leaving behind?

2. What do you want to become?

3. What resources will you use to create your vision?

4. What will you use to judge your progress?

5. Are you being patient and supportive of your hard work?

Step Six: Finding Witnesses and Support

Most people are not naturally loners. Their personalities are formed by the responses of people they are dependent on as children and are honed throughout their lives. To change deeply set dysfunctional behavior patterns, most people need to surround themselves with empathetic and supportive people who champion their new behaviors, and avoid those people who might be more comfortable with their old behaviors.

As you try to transform old behaviors into newer ones, you may often feel unsure of your footing. This is when you need impartial, loving witnesses to help keep you on track.

You will want to find people who can be as close to objective with you as possible. You want those people around you to remind you—without placation, indulgence, or criticism—of your new promises to yourself. If you are currently in a relationship, you might hope your partner will help you. If you are not involved with someone right now, or you're with someone who is too angry or disappointed to help, you will need to find support elsewhere.

Once you have identified a behavior that must be changed, legitimate witnesses will keep you honest. They will stay conscious of your taproots, help you identify your triggers, and remind you of your current vulnerabilities. Ideally, everything you say or do from now on should take you closer to the new behavior you want to master.

ESTABLISHING CRITERIA

Your witnesses must be able to do the following:

- Support your commitment.

- Allow you to find your own way.

- Stay honest.

- Remind you of your promises to yourself.

- Stay objective.

- Keep their own needs out of the way.

Step Seven: Staying Focused

Even though you are fully committed to challenging your deep-set behavior problems, you may find yourself backsliding at times. The person you have decided to become is still forming, and the person you were will hold on to old behaviors. If you occasionally find yourself behaving in old ways, you must be patient and forgiving. The old adage is correct: it doesn't matter how many times you fall, only that you get up again.

Eventually your new behaviors will become more automatic. Rely on your cheering squad to keep you from giving up and to remind you of the rewards that lie ahead, and don't put yourself down if you have temporary setbacks.

THE SABOTAGING PARTNER

The least understood but most probable barrier to accomplishing your goal may be the reaction of your current partner. In most cases, partners will be hopeful about positive changes, but in some cases, your partner's own negative behavior problems may reinforce yours, causing reciprocal damage. If you've always chosen the same kind of person and your relationships have never worked, your current partner may be consciously or unconsciously sabotaging you.

If you keep picking people who hurt you in the same way, you may be unconsciously seeking to symbolically reconnect with someone from your past. Perhaps you have believed that you can change what happened in the past by having more power in the present. Familiarity is a magnetic seduction, even when it leads you down the wrong path.

There are times when both partners choose each other as symbolic parents from the past. The result can be a mutual healing when both people are aware of the overlapping dysfunction, or it can be a total disaster if both partners reinforce old negative patterns.

STAYING ON TRACK

To stay on track, you will want to commit to these objectives:

1. Keep your eye on whom you want to become, but don't punish yourself when you slip back.

2. When you are in danger of slipping, reach out to your support system.

3. Make sure your partner is not sabotaging your efforts to change.

4. Reward yourself for successes.

5. Go easy on yourself if you're not always on target.

BATTLE SCARS AND HEROISM

Past failures may make you gun-shy about trying again. But as you replace destructive behaviors with those that build great connections, you will gain confidence in a new and more positive future. Confidence comes from the battle scars of heroism, and these battles are winnable. Faith is the belief that the improbable can transform into the possible. Trust is what you will feel in yourself, and in the future, when your efforts are rewarded.

Make the failures of the past a platform for your future success. Here are some guidelines:

1. Be courageous in exploring you childhood roots and relationship failures.

2. Set up your goals for alternative behaviors and practice them religiously.

3. Check in with yourself regularly to make sure that the child within you feels supported and cared for.

4. Keep your eye on what's possible, even when you feel lost.

5. Make sure your support network is intact.

6. Choose partners and friends who are compassionate but still hold you to your goals.

REMEMBERING THE BIGGER PICTURE

As you work on your goals, it will help to focus on others who have made it to the other side. Remember that no relationship is without heartbreak or misunderstanding. Everyone brings both positive and negative baggage into a relationship. New lovers always want to stay in love, and even though many relationships may fail, most people continue to seek a lasting commitment.

Relationship saboteurs desire love and commitment just like everyone else. Unfortunately, they repeat negative patterns of behavior that continue despite the alienation they create. Of course, destructive behaviors are not exclusive to saboteurs. Any of us are capable of behaving in these ways at some point in our lives. There were moments when these very human responses seemed reasonable and even justifiable. What sets saboteurs apart is the predictability, frequency, and intensity with which these behaviors occur and their consistently harmful effects on relationships.

To help you remember your goals, place these five reminders someplace where you can read them each day of your life:

- Reach for success in small steps along the way.

- Don't let failures stop you from trying again.

- Focus on the couples you know who have overcome similar challenges.

- Believe in your own capacity to care for the child within you.

- Remember that your sabotaging behaviors are not all of you.

In the following chapters, you will be given challenging exercises to help you leave your sabotaging behaviors behind. Some will be easier than others, but they are all an important part of the process. Sometimes sharing the exercises with a partner or close friend will make them more meaningful, while at other times you will feel better keeping them private. Sometimes you will notice changes in your behavior beginning very early in your practicing. At other times, the changes may come days or weeks later. Occasionally a lover or good friend will tell you about a wonderful difference in you that you hadn't noticed. These seven steps will work. Stay committed to your process and have faith in the outcome.

Insecurity:
"Will You Love Me Forever?"

Insecurity is the emotional experience of anticipated loss. People who are driven by it often feel vulnerable, unstable, and uncertain of their worth. The anxiety that accompanies insecurity is relentless. It is the fuel that drives jealous desperation. Trying to soothe the terrible anticipation of being discarded, people often act in ways that rob them of their self-respect and destroy the love they want so much to give and receive.

If you have sabotaged your relationships by being too insecure, you have known the humiliation of being perceived as too needy. You are familiar with your partner's patronizing words when he or she is worn down by your repeated need for reassurance.

Rather than feeling more valued, insecure people feel more anxious about their worth as their relationship deepens. The more intimate their attachment becomes, the more they may fear losing their partner to someone else. As that fear intensifies, their insecure behavior increases and they gradually end up pushing their partner away. The anticipation of loss fills their minds and hearts, and incessant self-doubt begins:

- "Will my partner stay in love with me?"

- "What if my partner loses interest?"

- "Could someone steal my partner from me?"

- "If I don't know where my partner is, could there be something going on that I don't know about?"

- "If every secret is not shared, am I in for a negative surprise?"

- "If we haven't made love in a week, does that mean sex with me is no longer appealing?"

- "Is the argument we had last night the beginning of the end?"

If you have suffered from those kinds of fears, you may have fallen into the trap of becoming a relationship sleuth, obsessively checking out every detail of your partner's life to ease your own anxiety. Then, turning any questionable finding into challenge and control, you may have driven your partner to leave the relationship.

If insecurity has dominated your relationships, you are not alone. Many people find themselves unable to stop this sabotaging behavior. Often, they are not aware of their partner's growing resentment until the relationship is well under way. Love is abundant when relationships are new, and insecurity is temporarily quieted when reassurance is plentiful. But as that early devotion decreases, insecure people begin to feel those haunting memories of eventual rejection. As their need for reassurance increases, their fear of loss becomes a self-fulfilling prophecy.

THERE IS HOPE

The good news is that, no matter where your insecurities originated, you can heal them. You can learn to manage your anxiety and change the patterns that have kept you from getting the love you deserve. Ultimately, your comfort will come from believing in your own value and having faith that love can last. Your worst enemy has been your fear of loss. Your greatest friend will be yourself.

THE SEVEN STEPS TO RECOVERY

To leave your relationship-sabotaging behavior behind, you will need to understand it more clearly, learn where your behavior began, and master the skills that will help you heal. The seven steps to recovery and the exercises that accompany them will be your healing plan.

Step One: Observing Your Insecure Behavior Without Judgment

To help you heal, you must first be able to identify your self-destructive behavior. You may need to recall painful or humiliating situations where your insecurity was the problem. As you recall these situations, you may feel embarrassed or self-critical. Remember, allowing yourself to give in to self-judgment will inhibit your ability to learn. Your goal in this first step is to recall those past behaviors while remaining an impartial, compassionate witness.

EXERCISE: Watching from the Outside

This exercise will help you remember times when you needed reassurance and your partner seemed burdened by your request. Remember to observe without criticizing how you acted. If you feel tempted to be self-critical, try to replace those feelings with compassion.

Recall a specific interaction where you remember feeling anxious about your partner's commitment to the relationship and you needed reassurance. Using your journal, write down enough of the dialogue to capture the theme. Here's an example:

You:	I worry when you don't come home on time at night and don't call.
Your partner:	I can't always remember to call. Why are you so insecure?
You:	I just feel better if I know you're okay.
Your partner:	You're just worried that I'm up to something. You need to get off my back.
You:	Can't you just tell me everything's okay? Why do you have to make me feel bad?
Your partner:	You can't expect to control everything I do.

Write down as many dialogues like this one that you can recall either from an ongoing or a past relationship. After each dialogue, write down the answers to the following questions: How did you feel when you approached your partner? When you didn't get the reassurance you needed, what did you do? What happened as a result? How did you feel about the way you reacted? How did your partner feel about you?

If you are down on yourself for exposing your anxious behaviors, can you let those feelings of self-judgment go? Sometimes writing about your feelings will help you separate them from the task of objectively answering the questions. Try to focus on what you are learning rather than on any negative feelings you may have about yourself while doing this exercise.

COPING WITH ANXIETY

Reliving these interactions may bring back the anxiety you felt during the original dialogues. Anxiety is always present when insecurity emerges. You are producing adrenaline as a way of dealing with your fear. Here are some physical symptoms of anxiety:

- heart racing

- tummy upset

- tingling in your hands or feet

- difficulty swallowing

- sweating

- feeling shaky

- feeling cold or hot

- pain in your chest

- feeling out of your body

Knowing that these physical responses are normal when you are anticipating loss can help you stay focused. Your symptoms can range from mild to severe, depending on how insecure you feel. They can appear in any combination and happen again whenever you re-create a memory or have a new experience.

EXERCISE: Checking Your Own Anxiety Symptoms

Looking back at the dialogues you recalled in the previous exercise, write down the situation you were responding to and any symptoms of anxiety you remember feeling. Here's an example:

It was two in the morning, and my partner hadn't come home and didn't call. I felt my heart start to race as if I were going to faint. I started to perspire and I couldn't breathe. I couldn't stop crying. I felt shaky.

Ask yourself if your physical reactions are typically the same whenever you feel insecure. If you can anticipate your anxiety symptoms, you can keep them from getting out of hand. You will be able to handle your anxiety with more confidence.

The most consistently helpful way to help decrease anxiety is to learn to control your breathing. The triangle between your shoulders and your solar plexus is where you store fear. Insecurity creates tension there and in your throat, and the adrenaline in your body will make you breathe faster.

To breathe correctly during a crisis, you must practice proper breathing habits when you are not feeling threatened or stressed. The more you train your body to breathe correctly, the better you will be able to control your breathing when you need to.

EXERCISE: Using Breathing to Quiet Your Anxiety Symptoms

Imagine the energy that's around your heart and imagine dropping it below your navel. Breathe in deeply and then allow your breath to completely exhale. Don't breathe again until your body asks you for its next breath. Drop your shoulders and relax your hands and feet. Feel the muscles in your body start to relax. Extend your tummy as you allow the breath to expand your lower lungs. Breathe deeply, gently, and rhythmically, as if you were enjoying something that made you calm and serene.

Teach your body that you are in control of your breathing and can command its rhythm when you need to hold insecurity at bay.

Step Two: Finding the Taproots of Your Insecurity

To find the origins of your insecurity, you need to follow the taproots to your earliest memories of feeling insecure. Those early experiences are driving your current insecure patterns. When you are able to relive them in the moment, you can change the way they influence your present relationships.

You may also have some inherited proclivities that make you more susceptible to anxious responses. Those tendencies are helped or hindered by the way your family may have responded to them. If you had any of the following distresses when you were small, you may have to work a little harder at learning to self-soothe as an adult:

- It was difficult for you to separate from loved ones, even for pleasurable activities.

- You were overly concerned with potential disaster.

- You seemed to need repeated comfort and reassurance.

- You were afraid to be far away from those you felt could protect you.

- You were upset if something unexpected occurred.

- You didn't like surprises.

- You had a hard time if you were forced to end one experience and shift quickly to a different one.

- You developed complicated rituals to feel in control.

- You worried intensely if something negative was in the foreseeable future.

Children who are born with innate anxiety but are fortunate enough to grow up in a family that responds with patience and kindness are more likely to learn how to keep it from running their emotional lives. Because you have identified yourself as an anxious relationship saboteur, you may have grown up without that kind of support. You may have, instead, had caretakers who mocked, minimized, or threatened you when you were legitimately upset. If so, you may be more at the mercy of your anxious reactions when you feel similarly threatened in your adult relationships.

Anxious children whose insecurities are intensified don't develop an internal advocate to rely on when they are frightened as adults. If you feel that your anxiety is harming your adult relationships, you may need to create that advocate in the present to help you gain control.

EXERCISE: Creating an Internalized Advocate

The goal of this three-part exercise is to help you create the internal advocate that you did not develop as a child.

Part 1: Recall one of your earliest memories of an especially threatening challenge. Pick an experience when you were anxious and couldn't take care of yourself. Try to remember as many details of the experience as you can and how you felt at the time. Take your time. Now, answer these questions in your journal: What was the challenge you were facing? How did you feel? What did you do? How did the people around you help or hinder you? What did you do and feel as a result of their intervention? Here's an example:

> I was in the third grade, scared to go out to recess because of a mean kid who kept teasing me. I felt stupid and ashamed. I pretended I had to wait for the teacher and couldn't leave the area. No one helped me. I didn't know what to do. I didn't want to go to school. I told my mom and dad, but they said I was just letting that kid scare me and I should just stand up to her. I tried and she hit me. I'm still scared of confrontation.

Part 2: Using the same memory, imagine that a significant person in your life stood behind you when you took on that challenge. Would you have responded differently with that kind of support? Here's an imagined scenario:

My dad came to school the next day and walked out to the playground with me. I showed him who the bully was. He held my hand and we went over to confront her. My dad told her to leave me alone, or he would report her to the principal. She looked afraid of him and said she was just playing with me. I felt stronger and told her she wasn't telling the truth. Suddenly, I wasn't afraid of her. I saw my dad step back and let me take over. I felt more confident than I ever had. I wasn't going to let her scare any other kids either.

Part 3: Compare your feelings in the two lists. This last part of the exercise is crucial to set your fantasy internal advocate in place.

You'll want to practice several of these imaginary exercises until you trust your new internal advocate to be there for you when you need it. Pick a new memory each time, and do this exercise until you feel confident that you have replaced those past memories of defeat with your newfound courage.

Step Three: Identifying the Triggers of Your Insecurity

Triggers are experiences that activate memories of significant events in your life. Sometimes the memories will be of extended situations, like living with an angry, alcoholic parent. At other times, they will be of a one-time event, such as the traumatic breakup of a relationship. Any behavior or personality characteristic of a lover can operate as a trigger if it reminds you of someone from your past.

You cannot always identify a trigger by its obvious similarity to a past event, but you can always identify it by your body's reaction to it. When your insecurity has been triggered, you're likely to feel more needy, demanding, frightened, clingy, empty, emotionally hungry, out of control, or anxious. Your mind may tell you that your dependency on your lover's availability is immature, but you won't feel able to stop your insecure reaction. Your self-respect may spiral downward and your partner may begin to withdraw, adding to your terror. Your feelings may set off physical symptoms of anxiety, making it all the more difficult for you to gain control over your emotional responses.

EXERCISE: Connecting Your New Advocate to the Present

In the previous exercise, your task was to replace childhood experiences of insecurity and anxiety with imagined responses that felt more positive. Doing this, you learned to face threatening events with courage and strength. Your goal now is to bring that new learned behavior into the present.

Pick an adult relationship in which your insecurity played a part in the relationship's failure. Recall and write down an interaction with your former partner when you felt you couldn't let go of your fears of loss. Next, rewrite the dialogue as you might have reacted if your internal advocate were in place. Here's an example of the first dialogue:

You: You hardly ever say you love me anymore.

Your partner: I tell you all the time. You never seem to hear it enough.

You: You don't seem to have any emotion in your voice.

Your partner: What do you need, some kind of script?

You: Maybe you're just pretending.

Your partner: Are you calling me a liar?

You: Please don't be mad at me. I'm sorry I said anything.

Here is the way the interaction might have looked if you had used your new inner advocate:

You: You hardly ever say you love me anymore.

Your partner: I tell you all the time. You never seem to hear it enough.

Inner advocate: Don't feel invalidated. Just tell him who you really are rather than what he is implying you are.

You: I know I rely on words more than you do, but I love to hear them.

Your partner: I'm not a verbal kind of guy; you know that.

Inner advocate:	Just accept his self-description and ask him directly if something has changed.
You:	Sometimes I can't read you very well and it makes me wonder if something's changed in how you feel about me.
Your partner:	Don't worry. Everything's great.
Inner advocate:	You can relax. You're doing great. Tell him how much you appreciate his reassurance, and offer what he needs.
You:	I feel so much better. I'll do my best to understand that your actions show me how you feel, but I'd also love it if you could sometimes tell me. The words are so important. And let me know if there's anything I can do to help you feel more loved, too.

It's perfectly okay to ask your partner for what you need, as long as your security is not dependent on his or her response. Hopefully, you now have a compassionate supporter inside you who will support you if your partner cannot.

Step Four: Examining When You Are Most Susceptible to Insecurity

Your susceptibility to triggered memories will depend on your current level of stress and your physical and emotional resources. Remember that anxiety is always present when insecurity emerges. Fatigue, illness, loss, physical or emotional imbalance, work pressures, lack of emotional support—all can hamper your ability to stay calm when your partner's actions feel threatening. The more stressed, tired, ill, or lonely you feel, the more likely you are to react strongly to any perceived peril.

If possible, you will want to put off situations that are likely to trigger your sabotaging behavior if you know you are already stressed. You can evaluate your susceptibility to triggers if you check in regularly with the following five important dimensions of your humanness:

Physical: As you go through the different parts of your body, do you feel any places that are tired, achy, or fragile?

Emotional: Do you feel as if you matter, that you have places to go to be nurtured, and that you are not alone?

Spiritual: Do you feel a greater purpose that supports you when you need it?

Mental: Do you feel alert, engaged, and intellectually challenged?

Sexual: Are you able to feel sensual and sexually responsive when you have adequate and appropriate stimulation?

EXERCISE: Checking Out Your Current Resiliency

To begin practicing, briefly write in your journal how you currently feel within each of these dimensions. Here's an example:

Physical: "I feel unusually tired today. Didn't sleep well. A little irritable."

Emotional: "I feel sad. Can't go out tonight because of too much work. Disappointed."

Spiritual: "I wish I could feel part of something bigger. It would make me feel less alone."

Mental: "I've been clicking at work lately. Very creative."

Sexual: "I'm feeling touch deprived. Would really like to have loving arms around me now."

Make it a habit to practice this exercise every day for a while. Each time you do, you'll be more in touch and better able to predict your responses. If you feel off-kilter, this would be a good time to be your own compassionate advocate and protect yourself from unnecessary challenges. When your reserves are down, you are much more likely to be at the mercy of your insecurity and more susceptible to the triggers that activate it.

If you're in a vulnerable place, your new commitments will feel a little shaky, and old patterns will be more likely to reemerge. Sometimes you'll just need to take a break until you feel a little stronger. As long as you maintain your commitment to change, you'll get where you want to go. Eventually practice will pay off, and you'll maintain your balance during critical situations.

EXERCISE: Predicting Your Insecure Responses

The goal of this exercise is to highlight those times when your needs are greater than your partner is willing to meet so that you are better prepared to take care of yourself.

Think of a time in a relationship when you knew you were down, but you fell prey to a negative interaction with your partner. Write in your journal whether you were overstressed, slightly stressed, or relaxed before the interaction. Then answer the following questions: What was going on before the interaction occurred? Can you recall if you felt unfulfilled, stressed, ill, or tired when the sequence began? What did you do? What happened between you and your partner? Where could you have stopped the sequence that pushed your partner away? How could you have avoided that interaction until your resources were more abundant in the situation?

Here's an example:

> I missed going to the gym this morning. I was looking forward to
> some sushi with my partner, but my business meeting ran late.
> I called him to ask if we could meet later. He said no, he would
> rather go to the gym instead and meet me later at home. I felt really
> disappointed, but didn't say anything. When I got home, I tried to
> make myself feel better by calling a friend. My partner still wasn't
> home, and I was beginning to get frustrated.
>
> I decided to make a great dinner, but when my partner got
> home, he said he wasn't hungry and just wanted to watch TV.
> I tried to get him to talk to me, but he said he was tired. I felt
> terrible, like I was in the way and unimportant. I felt like I did
> when I was a kid. My partner was acting like my dad, who never
> had time for me. I exploded and started a fight. He told me I was
> crazy and he wasn't interested in listening to a nutcase again.
> I felt devastated.

Instead of needing to be reassured by my partner, I realize I could have gone to the gym and worked out, called a good friend to spend some time with me, or taken a warm bath and gone to bed early to get some rest.

When you do this exercise, be sure to ask yourself if and when you could have intervened to prevent the cascade. If you do this exercise several times, you will be better able to think of your intervention before you risk responding with your loss-creating behavior.

Step Five: Learning to Be Confident and Calm Under Threat of Loss

Having explored your reasons for your insecurities in your past relationships and identified what they are, you will be ready to take better care of yourself in the future. Here are some promises you must make to yourself:

- "I will do everything I can to live fully in the present."

- "I will pay attention to my level of resiliency and stress, and do all I can to avoid conflicts when I am too vulnerable to handle them well."

- "I will practice and master my breathing exercises, and be in touch with how I am feeling and thinking so that I can maintain my self-control."

- "I will learn what current triggers activate my insecurities in my adult relationships."

- "I will watch myself carefully so that I can predict and avoid the emotional cascades that have pushed my partner away in the past."

- "I will try to associate only with those people who don't mock, threaten, or criticize me for being insecure."

- "I will rely on my own self-encouraging inner advocate when my partner cannot reassure me."

- "I will not beat myself up when I slip into old patterns."

EXERCISE: Checking In

Each evening, take a few minutes to ask yourself how you are doing on each of the promises you have made to yourself. Refrain from self-chastising if you aren't keeping up perfectly with each one. Checking in is only a way to make sure you are thinking about your goals. Caring this much about yourself will help you build more self-appreciation, which will help your internal advocate gain strength.

Step Six: Finding Witnesses and Support to Build Self-Confidence

You have known the pain of being rejected when you most needed reassurance from your partner. Unless your partner is ready to work with you in your new commitments, it would be better to search for the support you need from friends who understand you and won't feel burdened as you learn your new skills. Check in with them regularly and let them know how you are doing on your promises to yourself. The people you choose for your support team must be compassionate and objective, helping you develop your sense of security without indulging you in responses that may weaken it.

There are two main ways to start to build a strong support network. The first is to join a group of people who have suffered in the same way you have. There are many groups advertised on the Internet that deal with anxiety in relationships. Local churches also regularly sponsor self-help groups. Mental health agencies or individual professionals in your area may host groups that specifically address relationship problems that include problems with anxiety and insecurity. Because these groups frequently change sponsors, times, and locations, you'll need to continue searching until you find the right group for you.

Step Seven: Staying Focused

From time to time, you are bound to slip back into your sabotaging behaviors. Changing a lifetime of interactions doesn't happen overnight, and you must learn to forgive yourself if you don't improve immediately. Your genetic makeup and life experiences have both contributed to your situation, so it will take a while to sort things out.

Throughout your recovery process, you must remind yourself to believe that your hard work will pay off. You have to learn to trust in a future you cannot know, have faith in your own capabilities, and believe that others can help you achieve your goals. You can find the strength within yourself to leave your insecurities behind and live in the present moment, rather than in the fears of an unpredictable future and the regrets of an unalterable past.

Needing to Control: "I Run the Show"

There is not a single human interaction where the desire to control is absent. As very young children, we learn to use whatever influence we have to get others to do our bidding, even though we ultimately must submit to our parents' control over us. In each stage of our lives, we continue to dance the dance of who has the final say in each interaction.

Control issues are part of every adult relationship. All of us who are in relationships try to influence our partner in one way or another. If both partners in a relationship understand their mutual control needs and agree to help each other fulfill them, control conflicts aren't usually deal breakers. They become a problem when one partner compulsively needs to be in control and the other doesn't agree with the power structure.

HOW POWER AND CONTROL WORK TOGETHER
IN RELATIONSHIPS

How power and control work together in a given relationship defines the health or dysfunction of that partnership. The rules for power and control demonstrate not only how the relationship works but also how the partners feel about themselves and each other.

In a collaborative relationship, the rules are mutually created and open to renegotiation. After both partners agree on values, behaviors, and principles, either may take charge of any given situation when both believe it's in the best interests of the relationship.

Hierarchical relationships have the opposite structure. Only one of the partners has ultimate decision-making power, and that person creates the rules. By giving or withholding rewards or deciding on consequences, the partner in control wields that power until the other person refuses to participate or leaves the relationship. Most relationships are not purely one or the other type, but controlling relationship saboteurs seek partnerships that are closer to the hierarchical end of the continuum.

The partners of controlling people are initially attracted to them because of their personal confidence and ease at taking charge. If the controllers are also blessed with charisma, charm, status, or a great physical package, they may even get away with ruling most of their relationships for a while. The problem for controlling saboteurs is that most of their partners eventually grow tired of following rules that aren't open to negotiation. If the controlling partner cannot give up the need to control, the relationship usually begins a downhill slide.

REASONS FOR NEEDING TO CONTROL OTHERS

If you are a controlling relationship saboteur, you may have many personal reasons for choosing to be the way you are. You may not even realize that your need to have power over your partners is why they eventually leave you. But, to change your behavior, you'll need to understand what drives you to force each partner to submit to your will. Here are some possibilities:

- You grew up in a family of hierarchical control and feel it's your responsibility to follow that tradition.

- You're frightened that you won't get what you need unless you control the resources.

- You believe you will be controlled if you don't take charge.

- You should be in control because you do a better job.

- You're worried that you'll be held responsible if others don't do the right thing.

- You're often rewarded for taking charge.

- You think you can take better care of people than most others can.

- You like feeling powerful and managing others.

CONTROL AND INTIMACY

Many people are initially attracted to powerful people because they radiate confidence, a personality trait that can be alluring. A new partner may willingly accept a subservient role in exchange for being taken care of and enjoying surrendering to an exciting partner.

Romantic love is often depicted as a combination of a symbolic parent-child relationship and adult-to-adult lust. Seduction and control play a large part in love's early interactions. The partner who plays the role of the captured-and-cared-for one is likely to offer little resistance to initial conflicts but will later rebel against the limitations he or she originally accepted.

If you are a person whom others have initially deferred to but eventually leave, you may have been unable to let go of your power position when your partner wanted more say in the relationship. What was once a consensual power structure has probably deteriorated too often into the dynamic of a resented parental authority and a rebellious breakaway child.

Being in charge has its own sad liability. Those who insist on it may have never known the intimacy that can only occur in a relationship between equals. But you can learn to recognize where your need to control began and to let go of your fear of having someone else codirect the show. Once you do, you may experience a different kind of love than you've ever known.

THE SEVEN STEPS TO RECOVERY

Whether hurtful or revered, power hierarchies move through generations and continue to flourish unless they are successfully identified. As a controlling person, you more than likely used to observe controlling behavior or were once controlled the same way you now try to control your partners. To leave your relationship-sabotaging behavior behind, you will need to learn where it began and master the skills that will help you heal.

Step One: Observing Your Controlling Behavior Without Judgment

The first step is to identify the relationship rules that you live by now and how they have manifested in your relationships. As you explore them, try to remain neutral in your emotions. The goal of this exercise is simply to observe who you are without allowing yourself to negatively judge your behavior.

EXERCISE: What Are Your Rules?

Your rules are the "shoulds" in your life. Because you've insisted on the power position in your adult relationships, you will push to impose those "shoulds" on your partner. You will likely have one set of rules for yourself as the keeper of the power and another for your partner. In your journal, write an example of a separate list for each. Here is a sample:

RULES YOU LIVE BY

"Do your best at all times."

"Accept your responsibilities."

"Bear pain with dignity."

"Don't ask for help unless absolutely necessary."

"Take charge if you are the best to lead."

"Never quit."

"Keep things under control so that nothing goes wrong."

RULES FOR YOUR PARTNER

"Do what I say unless you have something better to offer."

"Make sure you understand before you challenge my decisions."

"If I'm taking care of you, don't complain about how I do it."

"Don't argue with the consequences if you mess up."

"Be grateful that I'm taking responsibility for the direction of the relationship."

"As long as you're with me, I make the rules."

"You can tell me what you want, but I make the final decision."

Your own rules will differ from the previous examples, but you are likely to see two very different sets of rules for yourself and your partner.

If, in this exercise, you seem less attractive to yourself than you would wish, let go of the self-criticism without changing what you've written. Rules can be wielded with compassion or with intimidation, and you may be a benevolent dictator rather than an intimidating one. Regardless, you must observe the one-way power hierarchy that exists and not allow yourself to be embarrassed by what you see.

Step Two: Finding the Taproots of Your Controlling Behavior

What we learn about power and control begins in the natural hierarchy children must live by. You have experienced the one-way power and control that is automatic between parents and children. To find the taproots of your sabotaging behavior, you will need to reach back to your earliest memories of controlling interactions.

EXERCISE: Identifying Your Childhood Authority Figure

Recall an adult in your childhood who exerted authority over you. Now think of an especially distressing dialogue that happened between you and that person as you were being disciplined. Whether this dialogue happened once or several times, it must be one that significantly affected you in a negative way.

Write down the scenario in your journal and be as detailed as you can as you answer the following questions: How old were you? What did you do wrong? Who is the authority figure and what relationship did you have with that person? What mood was he or she in? Where were you when you had this experience? What other people were present? What were your consequences? How did you feel? What did you wish had happened instead? Here's an example.

> *I was six years old. My grandmother called me into the kitchen. She took care of me while my mother was working. She was sometimes very angry and I was frightened of her when she was that way. No one else was there. I had forgotten to clean up the dog mess and she had stepped in it in the yard. She lectured me on how irresponsible I was and how I only thought of myself. She told me how important it was that I did what she told me to do, exactly how and when she told me to do it. I had to stay in my room with no TV for two hours and promise fifty times in my head how I wouldn't disobey her again. I felt angry and hated the way she talked to me. I wished my mom were there to take care of me instead.*

How do you feel after writing your own scenario? Does it help you to understand where your fear of being controlled may have begun? Can you see how you would never want to be controlled like that again?

When adults in relationships have ultimate authority over others, the children who watch them see them as all-powerful creatures who can do whatever they want. If they don't want to be controlled as adults, they conclude that the only other role to play is to become the dominant partner they observed. The crucial question for you as a control saboteur is have you treated your adult partners as you were treated in your memory scenario?

Step Three: Identifying the Triggers of Your Controlling Behavior

Certain triggers in your current relationships will set off your fear of being controlled and your need to take charge to keep that from happening. Eventually, you will learn to recognize these triggers as they occur and come up with alternative responses. But first you'll need to identify them.

EXERCISE: Connecting the Present to the Past

Recall a dialogue with an adult partner when you felt the need to control that person's behavior. In your journal, answer the following questions: What happened before you felt the need to take control? What did your partner do that made you want to take over? What did you do or say? How did your partner respond? What did you do? What happened to the relationship? How did you feel? How did your partner feel toward you? Here's an example:

> *My boyfriend and I were watching a game on TV, just hanging out on a Sunday afternoon. I asked him if he'd made the reservations for the show we wanted to see that night. He said he'd forgotten, but he'd do it later. I got really angry because he'd promised. I told him that he doesn't care about me and he's totally irresponsible. He got angry and called me a bitch. Said he wasn't my puppet and I could make my own stupid reservations, since they had to be done on my clock. I told him he had no right to be angry with me for his own mistake. Maybe he could come up with an idea of his own once in a while. He told me he didn't want to see me that night. I felt like I was right and he was wrong, and he should apologize. He told me he hates that part of me, but I had to show him what he had done wrong.*

When you complete your entry in your journal, look at the ways in which you sounded like the authority figure from your past and the ways in which your partner sounded like you did as a child. Were the verbal exchanges similar? If the words and emotions you exchanged feel familiar, your past may be infiltrating your present relationships. You'll want to look more closely at the triggers that set off your need to control.

Step Four: Examining When You Are Most Susceptible to Needing to Control

If you cannot give up control, you probably exhibit that behavior in other relationships in your life. You may be more sensitive in situations where you feel responsible for the outcome or are fearful that someone less capable will end up controlling you. The earlier you can recognize any conflict situations where you feel no other option but to control the interactions, the sooner you'll be able to change your responses.

EXERCISE: Control Checklist

In your journal, write down some interactive behaviors you can remember that automatically set off your need to control. The people on the receiving end of your reactions can be lovers, bosses, family, friends, service people, or any other authority or subordinate. Use the following format:

"When _____ does _____, I _____."

Here are some examples:

"When my girlfriend forgets to call me on time, I get really angry and tell her I don't like it. Sometimes I won't answer her next few calls, just to show her she can't do that to me."

"When my boss yells at me for not working hard enough, I feel like he doesn't know what he's talking about, so I usually ignore him and do what I want."

"When my mother tells me she wants more of my time, I tell her she's too demanding and should find something else to do. Then I don't call her for a month, so she knows who's in charge."

"When my best friend can't get the tickets he promised me, I tell him I can't count on him and I'll do it myself from now on. If I can't control him, I don't want to depend on him."

After writing in your journal, look for key words at the beginning that describe what triggered you. Next look for the key words that express how you judged the person you interacted with and how you justified taking control once you came to your conclusion.

Example: "When my girlfriend *forgets* to call me on time, I get really *angry* and *tell* her I don't like it. Sometimes I won't answer her next few calls, just to *show* her she can't do that to me."

Do this exercise as often as you need to get a good sense of what triggers show up the most frequently and what your most consistent responses are. You'll recognize the rules you internalized as a child and how you justify your controlling behavior when anyone breaks them.

Step Five: Learning How to Give Up Negative Control

If you have learned to be in control from negative childhood memories or you just have a naturally dominating personality, you will not find it easy to trust others to take the lead, even when you feel it's appropriate. Some of your behavior may have been even appropriate or appreciated in your past relationships. To go forward, you'll first want to separate the parts of your behavior that are not destructive from those that you want to leave behind.

EXERCISE: Distinguishing Behaviors

In your journal, first list what the important people in your life have liked about your controlling behavior. That may sound like an odd suggestion, but it's not. Here are some possibilities: responsible, vigilant, takes charge, knowing, capable, authoritative, powerful, effective, commanding, tenacious, attentive, caring. Now make a second list of what these same people have disliked about your controlling behavior. Here are some possibilities: bullying, dominating, dictatorial, manipulative, monopolizing, pushy, always running the show, subjugating, condescending, coldly functional.

The qualities of the first list are commonly perceived as positive when they coexist with respect and support. People with these qualities are open to suggestions and coleadership. The qualities on the second list are those of a dictator and will eventually destroy any good relationship.

Now make a third list. This list will show the qualities of take-charge people who aren't especially attached to their power over others. They just want the best person to lead and, if it happens to be them, they're happy to do it. But they're also willing to share power and even give it up if someone else can do a better job. Their qualities might include the following: receptiveness, mutuality, unity, support, harmony, reciprocity, cooperation, sympathy, curiosity, interest, reasonableness, kindness, logic.

From the characteristics you see in the first and third lists, create a combined list of the qualities you would enjoy in someone you would admire and respect. Add any others you feel are important. Create an imaginary person who embodies those qualities. This person will become your new role model and become part of your internal dialogue for the future. When you wonder if your take-charge behavior is likely to alienate your partner, ask your fantasy role model for feedback before you act.

The opposite of control is not submission. It's cooperation. Two people in an egalitarian relationship give power to each other without fear of being controlled. They use a combination of the qualities in the first and third lists to ensure that each partner will be both a strong leader and a comfortable follower in the same relationship.

EXERCISE: Replacing Your Childhood Authority

Your goal is to replace the authoritarian person from your past with one who uses authority in a supportive and encouraging way. Go back to step two, where you identified a painful disciplinary experience with an authority figure from your childhood. Now recall the same situation and replace that person with yourself as the authority figure. This time stay in touch with the child's feelings and teach the same lesson, but do it as the fantasy role model you created in the last exercise. Using the example from the exercise in step two, you might write instead:

> *I take care of my six-year-old grandson when his mother is working. He's a little bit lazy and forgets to do his chores, but he's a great kid. Sometimes I get a little irritable with him when he forgets to do what he promised, but I try to help him remember without making him feel bad about his mistakes. If I lose my temper, I always apologize and tell him how much I love him. I also have him participate in deciding his own consequences to help him remember and to reward him when he does a good job. I want him to know that he is loved even when he's in trouble. He will learn his lessons over time if he feels respected and cared for.*

How was your dialogue different from the dialogue you recalled in step two? How did the child feel in your new dialogue? Could you similarly replace your authority figure in your adult interactions with your partner and others? Do you think you can behave differently now in these relationships?

Step Six: Finding Witnesses and Support to Help You Give Up Negative Control

This step will be your most uncomfortable task. It may be hard for you to rely on others when you have always taken the responsibility for a relationship, and used power and control to keep it intact. You have probably known very few people in your life with whom you felt comfortable sharing power, and you probably have attracted people who didn't fight you for control or left you when you couldn't stop. Now you need to find people you can trust. Where will you look? What kinds of people can you listen to without activating your fear of being controlled?

You must look for witnesses for whom power is not an issue. These people not only seek and foster collaboration and cooperation in their relationships but also help each other by willingly sharing leadership. If they have to fight for what's right, they do, but the goal of those conflicts is the ultimate good of the relationship.

Such people are often found working for good causes. Though power-and-control hierarchies also exist in humanitarian organizations, most who serve them are united in a higher cause, and welcome cooperative participation and generous sharing of power and resources.

EXERCISE: Keeping Real Heroes in Sight

Are you familiar with anyone who connects with people without needing to exert power or control, yet is willingly followed? Great leaders for peace may come to mind, like Gandhi or Nelson Mandela, religious figures like Jesus, or philosophical giants like Socrates.

You may even have known an ordinary hero in your own neighborhood who has been highly influential in making a difference without the need to push his or ideas on others.

Reflect on those people who use their power and control over others with benevolence and commitment to a higher cause. These individuals can inspire you to give up the negative aspects of power and control, and still retain your right to be a leader when you and your partner agree you are the best to be in charge.

If possible, try to talk with any of these people about their values and approach to relationships. If the people you choose as role models are not available, you can have imaginary dialogues with them. They can even be people from your past who are no longer here.

These dialogues will help you experience a new way to respond to the triggers that have activated your need to control.

Step Seven: Staying Focused

Can you believe that you can live your life by inspiring and influencing your partners without needing to control them? What would you need to do to make that happen? Can you use your need to be in charge to make a difference in the world instead of pushing your partner to submit to your control? Would you value a partner who respects the positive aspects of your power and control but is strong enough to hold his or her own boundaries?

EXERCISE: New Goal Chart

Review the exercise in step four, where you found key words that describe what triggers you. List these words on the left side of a journal page. Leave the rest of the page blank.

Then, if you hear any of these trigger words during the course of a day, record next to these words in your journal what you felt at the time and if you were able to replace the need for control with one of collaboration.

Start fresh with a new page every day. Encourage yourself each day when you are able to stay nonreactive to your trigger words, and cross out each one as it loses its power to trigger you.

Exercises like this one will help you stay focused and hopeful. Though it may be hard to see when you are struggling, untold positives await you when you triumph over your sabotaging behavior. You'll attract partners who value your strengths and won't have to run from your weaknesses. You'll feel the relief of letting someone you trust take on some of the responsibilities for things that you used to feel only you could do. And, perhaps most importantly, you may one day know the comfort of being cared for by someone you don't need to control.

5

Fear of Intimacy:
"I Need You, but Not That Close"

Most people think of intimacy as a positive experience. From childhood on, it is the haven humans seek from isolation and loneliness. They have known its warmth and familiarity through connections with people that matter, and suffered its absence during times of separation.

Intimacy has many dimensions: With a trusted friend it's the experience of being known deeply, accepted, and enjoyed as a peer. With a child, intimacy feels both fragile and safe, watchful and unconditionally loving. With a lover, intimacy can be arousing, engaging, passionate, and sweet.

The desire for lovers to blend with each other is innate. It is a symbolic re-creation of the fusion new beings must feel in the safety and protection of the womb. Romantic love is fueled by the desire to feel that sense of unconditional inclusion again. Filling its partners with its chemical combination of testosterone and oxytocin, romantic love symbolically re-creates that fusion experience. Lovers willingly give themselves to one another, unconcerned about the surrender of physical independence that true intimacy requires.

WHEN INTIMACY HURTS

For some people, romantic fusion activates a totally different set of feelings. Those who fear it feel the same hunger for intimate connection that all people do, but the closer they get to it, the more they want to run away. Instead of the ecstasy that bonding offers, they feel terror, mistrust, anger, and debilitating fear.

Though there are many reasons why people fear intimacy, most often it is because they have experienced pain in their past intimate connections. Though betrayal can happen at any time of life, the most significant damage is done in childhood, when helplessness creates raw vulnerability.

Children who are abused, neglected, or emotionally erased have only known intimacy paired with pain or loss. They often grow into adults who cannot trust or sustain intimacy without expecting those negative feelings to resurface. These negative feelings may not show up in the relationship's initial stages, when there's enough emotional distance and a sense of control. But when their partner gets too close, they begin to feel suffocated, anticipating being captured and traumatized again. Driven by those fears, they push their partner away. Now separate and lonely, they may try to win back their partner and recapture the very intimacy from which they've fled.

People who are afraid of intimacy may eventually become commitment phobic, avoiding intimacy and long-term commitment. After multiple failures, they may talk about intimate relationships in these ways:

"Once I commit, I'll never be able to leave, even if I'm unhappy."

"I'll feel guilty and torn if I don't do what I'm asked."

"I may lose the option of finding someone better."

"I will risk being abandoned."

"I'll feel trapped."

"I'll be controlled."

"I'll be obligated to be what someone else wants me to be."

"I'll hurt someone."

"I'll forget who I am."

All of these explanations for avoiding intimacy have a common core: the anticipation and certainty that intimacy will result in exploitation.

THE PARTNERS OF INTIMACY SABOTEURS

If you are an intimacy saboteur, you may not experience any fear early on in your relationship. In fact, in the beginning, you are likely to be eager to connect, warmly responsive and seemingly okay. Then, often without warning, you may begin to feel cornered, irrationally blaming your partner for superficial mistakes.

When you have pushed your partner away, he or she has probably reacted with confusion and resentment, tried hard to reconnect, and pushed you farther away. Your rejecting behavior can also increase your partner's clinginess. Most people will try harder when they've been trained to expect intimacy and then lose it without explanation.

Once successful in getting your partner to finally give up and leave the relationship, you have most probably used your well-honed reentry seduction to promise your partner a positive outcome the next time around. If your partner loved you enough to try again, you were given the opportunity to play out that cycle for a while. But eventually, unless your partner is willing to tolerate this pull-in–push-away behavior, he or she will eventually move on.

EVALUATING YOUR ABILITY TO SUSTAIN INTIMACY

The following questions will help you determine if you are an intimacy saboteur:

- Do you begin relationships wanting to be intimate and then run when your partner gets too close?

- Do you use words like "needy," "dependent," "pushy," or "controlling" to describe your partner when you need to create distance?

- When your partner expects more commitment, do you start to find fault with him or her?

- In your love relationships, do you seek closeness and then destroy it?

- Do you find that the more emotionally distant you are from your partner, the more you miss him or her?

- When you begin to feel dependent on your lover, do you push her or him away?

- Do you avoid your fears by only connecting with unavailable partners or those you can easily dump?

- Do you frequently test your partner's love?

- When your relationships end, are you likely to feel a mixture of relief and grief: glad you can't be hurt anymore and saddened that you have again pushed away the love you need?

If you sincerely want to be in a committed relationship but fear holds you back, please take heart. Fear of intimacy can be conquered. With a caring partner who respects your conflict and doesn't take it personally, you can learn to set clearer boundaries and enjoy the comfort of closeness without the fear of being engulfed.

THE SEVEN STEPS TO RECOVERY

Overcoming your fear of intimacy requires both respecting the reasons for your responses and challenging yourself to face them. Acting in the face of your fears takes courage and faith, but you will succeed if you stay on track.

Step One: Observing Your Fear of Intimacy Without Judgment

As an intimacy-phobic lover, you have most likely pushed many partners away. Those losses may have left you feeling inadequate as a long-term partner and sad about the people whom you have rejected along the way. Be careful to avoid self-criticism as you observe past behavior, for judging yourself will only hamper your efforts to understand it.

EXERCISE: Separating Your Desire for Intimacy from Your Need to Run

Pick one of your adult relationships where you remember inviting your lover into ever-increasing levels of intimacy before you hit a wall where you had to push that person away. Using your journal, make two lists. The first will be statements you've made to your partner when you were excited about your relationship. The second will be the reasons you used to back off when the relationship got too close. Here are some sample lists:

GETTING CLOSE

"I'm so comfortable with you."

"You're so easy to talk to."

"I love spending time with you."

"I really like your friends."

"I've never known anyone as interesting as you are."

"I love the way you cuddle."

"You never ask too much of me."

BACKING AWAY

"You're too needy."

"I don't feel like talking."

"I need some time to myself. I never get anything done anymore."

"Your friends are too demanding."

"Can you talk about something that actually interests me?"

"I feel closed in. Can you sleep on the other side of the bed?"

"I can't keep up with all your requirements."

"You're asking too much lately."

You may find yourself feeling embarrassed as you compare your two lists. That's understandable. Without putting yourself down, keep exploring your thoughts and feelings. When you look at the statements you made as you were backing away, were you internally aware that you were not trying to break up with your partner? Were you just feeling cornered and in need of some space? Most probably, the relationship hadn't changed, but your ability to handle the intimacy had met its limit.

What's missing is how you got from comfort to fear. The place to look is where that transition to fear began.

Step Two: Finding the Taproots of Your Fear of Intimacy

If you've been practicing run-away behavior for a long time, you may have never thought about what earlier traumas may be triggered by your present experiences. If you can find the connections, changing your responses will become easier.

BOUNDARY VIOLATIONS

All children seek intimacy. They crave the comfort of the arms that protect and encourage them when they are small. As they grow more independent, they explore the outside world, knowing they can return to that safety when they need it. In a healthy environment, children thrive from the opportunity to alternate between fusion and independence, and they grow up to be adults who are comfortable with both.

When parents use their children to fill their own hungers or satiate their own needs, they control their children's choices and may force them into sustained intimacy or prolonged isolation. Unable to choose what's natural, those children lose their ability to set healthy boundaries and grow up to later avoid intimacy totally, over-sacrifice to attain it, or bounce wildly between the two extremes.

The following parental emotional or physical behaviors are the most common contributors to boundary confusion in children: demands for excessive closeness; inappropriate touch; living vicariously through the

74

child; brainwashing; restricting independence; teaching obligations that are not beneficial to the child. The result of those infractions will be a child who learns that his or her needs for intimacy or natural desire for separation will be controlled and contaminated by those who are supposed to care.

EXERCISE: Have Your Boundaries Been Violated?

Recall a person from your childhood who violated your need for intimacy and prevented you from separating when you felt entrapped. This person could have been a family member, teacher, coach, friend, or babysitter—anyone who had access to you on a regular basis. Note: you may want to recall a relationship that wasn't too painful. Trauma is better left until you have become more familiar with this exercise. Now re-create a scene where you can remember how that person took advantage of your helplessness to control your own boundaries. Remember if you tried to stop that person's behavior and what happened. Ask yourself if others who witnessed the interactions condoned or condemned them.

When you have the scene clearly in mind, write down the situation in as much detail as you can remember, as if it were happening now. These questions may help: How old are you at the time? Who is the person? What's happening? Are you trying to change the situation? What's the result? Is there anyone there who can help you? How do you feel when that person fails to help? What can you do afterward? Does the same sequence repeat? What are you told to do or feel about the interaction? The following is an example of what you might write:

> I've just turned seven and it's summertime. My parents have sent
> me to my aunt's house so they can go on a vacation. Though I don't
> mind visiting, I don't like to spend a lot of time with her because she
> won't leave me alone.
>
> At the beginning of vacation, I'm enjoying my time with her
> because we do fun things, but after a while, she starts to bug me
> again. She wants me to eat meals with her and watch her television
> programs, snuggle close on the couch. I feel smothered.
>
> When I try to get away to play by myself, she follows me
> around. I try to tell her I want to be alone, but she pouts and then
> won't talk to me. I'm scared that she won't love me anymore, so I try

to do what she wants. I have to stay for two weeks, and by the end of the time, I hate her.

On my last day there, I have a tantrum and tell her I never want to see her again. She gets very angry and tells me I have bad manners and I don't appreciate how much she loves me. I feel guilty and angry and don't want to go back, but I know I will miss her when I get home.

When you think about the person from your past, what are his or her main characteristics? Here are some possibilities: funny, exciting, loving, possessive, self-centered, too clingy, invasive, wanting too much, punishing, angry, lecturing, making you feel guilty.

Think of as many characteristics as you can, writing them down in your journal. Can you see how this person's positive characteristics could pull you back into the relationship and the negatives could push you away? Ask yourself if you currently choose partners who resemble this person from your childhood. Do you act like this person in your current relationships when you want intimacy and your adult partner doesn't?

You can use this exercise to explore more traumatic episodes. Painful memories carry more intense emotions. When you can recall and understand what happened, your capacity for healing will increase.

Step Three: Identifying What Triggers Your Fear of Intimacy

To pinpoint your transition from lover to rejecter, you'll need to know when your intimate and separating behaviors are most likely to occur. Your sabotaging behavior may seem to be related to your partner's behavior, but your seemingly irrational switch from welcome to rejection is much more likely to come from an internal, growing fear that you've been unable to recognize. You will be able to recognize a pattern when you look at your past relationships more closely.

EXERCISE: Tracking Your Past Relationships

Recall three significant adult relationships. In your journal, write the names of the partner in each relationship. For each relationship, answer the following questions:

1. What about that person attracted you?

2. What did you do to bring that person close to you?

3. How intimate did the relationship become?

4. How long did it last before you needed to separate?

5. How did your feelings change toward that person?

6. What reasons did you give to justify your separation?

7. How did you convince the person to reconnect?

Now, looking at your answers, compare your behavior with each partner. For example, you might have answered the first question in each case like this:

Partner 1: "She was flattered by my attention."

Partner 2: "She liked my directness."

Partner 3: "I felt confident and in control."

Do you see any patterns? Does the sequence feel familiar? Can you see any similarities between these adult relationships and the relationship from your childhood that you recalled in the previous exercise?

Sometimes the similarities may not be immediately obvious. The more often you do this exercise, the more you will be able to see them. Eventually, you'll also be able to anticipate them in your relationships.

Step Four: Examining When You Are Most Susceptible to Fear of Intimacy

You can anticipate when your fear of intimacy will emerge by looking at three areas of susceptibility in your adult relationships:

- What triggers do you typically associate with your past partners?

- How do you lead your partners to expect intimacy that you cannot sustain?

- Where else in your life do you set up situations where you promise more than you can deliver?

EXERCISE: Identifying the Three Areas of Your Susceptibility

Name your triggers. List in your journal any personality, behavioral, and physical characteristics that are typical of those partners who have activated your fear of intimacy. How have your partners behaved when you were close, and how did they react when you pushed them away and then pulled them close again? Here's an example of what you might write:

My partners are usually warm and receptive. They are physically and emotionally open and make themselves available to me whenever I want them. Unfortunately, they eventually all want more of my time. When I ask for space, they get upset and ask me what they've done wrong. They take it personally, and I usually agree with them so I can get some distance. I don't like blaming them, but it's easier that way. I'm not trying to end the relationship, but I have to act that way to get them to let go. I am pretty successful at getting them back if I don't wait too long.

Examine your pattern. If you keep seducing and disconnecting, and your partner keeps participating, he or she must take some responsibility for the continuing pattern. But you are responsible for any double messages that keep your partner guessing. Try to write a few lines in your journal that describe your intent when you start a relationship and your feelings when the relationship ends. You might write something like the following:

I've been looking for long-lasting love all my life. I really believe that I want a loving, affectionate relationship. I tell my partners that at the beginning of my relationships, and I'm sincere. I let them know that I've never been able to stay close for very long but that maybe they'll be the one who can help me fight my fears. When they finally get fed up with my inability to stay connected and they leave the relationship, I feel relieved but terrible. Some of them would have made great long-term partners, but I couldn't figure out how to make that happen.

Look at similar situations: If you are an intimacy-phobic person, you may also be alternating between closeness and distance with other people in your life besides your lovers. It's easier to mask those patterns when you aren't so closely connected, but they'll be clear if you look for them. Check your intimacy reservoir nightly and ask yourself how you're doing with every relationship in your life. You might write something like the following in your journal:

I give everything I've got in every new relationship: work, friends, workout partners. But as soon as they expect me to keep giving that level of involvement or escalate my commitment, I start to feel trapped and obligated. It seems as if everyone expects me to deliver at that level all the time, and I can't. I've created some pretty flimsy excuses to avoid delivering on my promises. I'm beginning to realize that I've probably disappointed a lot of people.

Remember, no self-criticism. You more than likely have had a good reason to behave the way you have. Focus on what you've learned about yourself and the fact that you're facing your own fears and you're ready to change.

Step Five: Learning How to Overcome Your Fear of Intimacy

Your goal is to create a sustainable intimacy with someone you love and who loves you. Hopefully, you have a greater understanding of where your boundary violations began. That will help you understand why you pick the partners you do, and how you alternately seduce and disconnect from them. Using that knowledge, you can now honestly inform your current partner about your patterns and work with that person to leave your old patterns behind.

EXERCISE: Your Transformation Chart

Rate the following statements of transformation on a scale of 1 to 5, where 1 = not at all; 2 = infrequently; 3 = when you really try; 4 = easily, if you stay in touch with your behavior; and 5 = automatically.

1. You can identify relevant traumatic experiences from your past.

2. You understand what you're attracted to in your partners.

3. You can tell your partner why you are afraid of intimacy and how you have run from it in the past.

4. You know which of your partner's behaviors activates your fears.

5. You can see relationships as possible havens rather than potentially traumatizing events.

6. You no longer blame your partners when you start to feel cornered.

7. You no longer create reasons on your own for disconnecting from your partners.

8. You can protect your own boundaries when you want to bring your partner close.

9. You can stop testing your partner to see how often you can get him or her to disconnect and come back again.

10. You no longer have to run away, and you can tell your partner what's going on when you are triggered.

Add up your score. This initial score is a baseline. Once a week, rate the statements again. If your score is going up, no matter how slowly, you're on your way to building new kinds of relationships and your fears will diminish. If it's going down, you may still be giving in to your old patterns, and need to reevaluate your behaviors and the partners you are choosing.

Step Six: Finding Witnesses and Support for Overcoming Fear of Intimacy

If you have been able to bring people close after pushing them away, you must possess many positive qualities. When you reach out to ask people to help you witness your own growth, you may be in danger of treating them as you have your past partners, seducing them as potential healers and afterward feeling too obligated to continue with the relationship. Be careful not to get too close to anyone too soon, at least until you are certain you can stay connected.

Whomever you choose as a witness, you'll want to be up front about the typical five stages of your personal interactions:

1. You use whatever charm, status, or appeal to get someone to want to be close with you.

2. You enter a gray area where you start to feel closed in and have second thoughts about staying connected.

3. You start to find fault with your partner and use those criticisms to drive the person away.

4. You use your original appeal to bring your partner back after you've reestablished your boundaries.

5. You feel grief and regret when the other person stops playing your game.

It will be easier to avoid slipping into your old patterns if you openly discuss each of these five stages with the person you've asked to help you change. Discuss your feelings and also how your behavior affects them. Some people practice this dialogue alone at first, with a fantasy partner, because the process can be embarrassing. But if you can find someone who knows you well, still cares for you, and has had these experiences with you in the past, that person will be a great mirror for you as you work through this process.

Step Seven: Staying Focused

Even though you are now equipped to recognize your patterns, new love relationships will activate both your longing for closeness and your fear of being trapped. You will need a powerful rationale to stay on target.

Driven in the past by your fears, you have most likely focused more on yourself than on your partner's reactions to you. Getting out of your own fear cycle can help you leave it behind. The last exercise is for you to go beyond your self-centered view, so you can give your partner what you wanted long ago, when your sabotaging behaviors were first created.

EXERCISE: Living in the Heart of Your Partner

In your journal, list your intimacy-avoidance behaviors in the order in which they typically occur, accompanied by what you believe your partner's experience has been when you acted that way. The following is an example:

You: I encouraged my partner to get close to me.

Your partner: I felt invited into an intimate relationship.

You: I wanted and desired my partner.

Your partner: I was encouraged and flattered by the attention.

You: I expressed my increasing devotion and love.

Your partner: I thought our love was flowering.

You: I felt secure and loved in return.

Your partner: I'm opening my heart.

You: I started to feel too connected.

Your partner: I noticed a slight pulling back.

You: I began looking for things to criticize.

Your partner: I felt slighted and blamed for things I didn't do.

You:	I escalated my disappointed and frustrated comments.
Your partner:	I started to push back, asking for reasons.
You:	I used the pushing as my final reason to separate.
Your partner:	I felt rejected, confused, and hopeless.
You:	I felt relieved but lonely, so I decided to try again.
Your partner:	I still felt love in my heart, so I accepted the offer.
You:	I started the cycle again.
Your partner:	I hoped it would work this time.

Seeing the effects you have had on your partners will help you look at your behavior through someone else's eyes. Taking care of your partner will help you reach back in time and heal the traumatized child within you at the same time. If you know how to pick partners who can understand the depth of your conflicts and not take them personally, you'll create relationships where fear is simply the stepping-stone to renewed trust.

Needing to Win:
"I Dare You to Challenge Me"

Need-to-win relationship saboteurs provoke their partners into verbal battles and end up with hollow victories. They argue their partners into submission or withdrawal, and they sacrifice intimacy in the process. These saboteurs lose friends and lovers with their compulsive, combative behavior. Whenever challenged, they cannot resist the opportunity to have the last word, no matter what the cost.

It's tempting to write off need-to-win saboteurs as self-centered, self-righteous people who don't care about alienating their partners. But if they didn't care, they would stand triumphant after each battle, righteous about their victories. To the contrary, they usually feel guilty about the damage they've caused and want to be forgiven.

The childhood memories of these saboteurs are often of dominating authority figures who taught them to compete as a way of life. Many people talk of parents and older siblings who modeled an environment where winning was the only alternative to humiliation. Many times, they painfully experienced the mockery that losing invited or the dangerous consequences of being conquered.

In their adult relationships, need-to-win saboteurs often use fighting as a prelude to intimacy. They fear that conflict is a necessary ingredient for passion. Unfortunately, over time, it too often becomes a substitute.

STOPPING THE CYCLE

If you cannot bear to let someone have the last word or are unable to stop advocating for your point of view, you will eventually drive your partner into passive submission or out of the relationship. Whatever positive attributes you initially brought to the relationship will be eventually eclipsed by your need to subordinate your partner's thoughts and feelings to your own.

You are at the mercy of your own need-to-win behavior if your after-battle mode is conciliatory and seductive, and you want your partner to agree that you've done nothing wrong. Is it typical for you to expect your partner to welcome your desires for immediate intimacy and to be surprised when that doesn't happen? Do you feel unfairly rejected if your desires are not reciprocated or are described as premature and inappropriate? Many need-to-win relationship saboteurs use their partner's after-battle withdrawal as a reason to begin another battle.

HOPE FOR CHANGE

Competition and winning have their place in relationships when both partners understand the rules and enjoy the game. They can enhance intimacy when both partners are on the same emotional team. But when the win becomes more important than the relationship, the outcome can be devastating.

Understanding where you learned to win at the expense of another can help you transform your competitive skills into positive relationship attributes. The key is moving from the concept of one winner and one loser to two people fighting together toward the same outcome.

A Word of Warning

Competitive people usually attract partners who give in, fight back, martyr themselves, or withdraw. But occasionally they are magnets for people who are looking for an unsuspecting vehicle for their own rage. If you have a history of attracting volatile people who rapidly escalate their anger when you argue with them, think seriously about whether it's worth it to be in that kind of relationship at all. You may be facing someone who is much more invested in winning than you are.

THE SEVEN STEPS TO RECOVERY

As you begin your seven steps to recovery, you may find your need-to-win behavior triggered by what is asked of you. Stay aware of any defensive or combative responses and try to let them go if they arise.

Step One: Observing Your Need-to-Win Behavior Without Judgment

Your first step in changing your behavior is to simply observe your typical behavior in past relationships. You're going to be looking at how your need-to-win behavior may have shifted during the relationship and what your partner's reactions were. If any defenses come up, try to let them go. You'll want to gather as much information as you can, and justifying your reasons for doing what you've done will only block the memories that you'll need to help you change.

Certain patterns of argumentative interaction will have dominated many of your past relationships and will become evident as you explore them. Do not focus on failure, and stay as honest as you can. Listen carefully to any negative inner dialogues that may arise. They could represent how you were spoken to as a child.

EXERCISE: The Three Stages of an Argumentative Relationship

Pick a romantic relationship where your competitive need to win played a significant part in its demise. Now separate the relationship into three stages:

Stage 1: Describe what your competitive arguments were like when the relationship was new.

Stage 2: Describe your arguments when the relationship had passed its honeymoon stage and you were more established.

Stage 3: If applicable, describe your arguments as the relationship neared its end.

Use the following questions about each stage to guide you: How did you feel toward your partner? What were most of your arguments about? What behaviors did you use to win? How often did these arguments occur? How long did they typically last? How did your partner feel toward you when they were over? How did you feel about yourself? Here's an example for stage 1:

We didn't argue about much, but when we did, it was short and sweet. We had so much fun together most of the time, and he was so easy to get along with that there wasn't much to fight about. Besides, I liked the confrontations because they usually got us aroused and then the sex was great. Once in a while, he would get a little demanding, like wanting to see certain friends I didn't like, but I could usually get my way. He rarely knew as much as I did about any subject, so he pretty much caved in when things got too upsetting. He liked my spunk and the fact that I was so informed. Sometimes he would brag to me that he was better at something than I was, but I could always talk him out of it. He usually forgave me because our intimacy was fantastic. I felt smart and important.

Here's an example for stage 2:

We started arguing more about less important things. He never seemed to remember to be on time or to call me when he said he would. I felt impatient and neglected. We'd fight about who said what at a party or whether or not he'd told me something. When we got into arguments, I told him I'd believe anything if it made any sense, but it never did. I had to keep telling him that he was wrong, because he was. He started telling me that I never listened to him and that I always had to be right. He was so wrong. Sometimes we would fight for hours over nothing. He'd finally say he'd had enough, and then we wouldn't make love for two days. I couldn't understand why he couldn't just accept that I paid more attention to things than he did.

Here's an example for stage 3:

He was finding more reasons to spend more time at work even when he was supposed to be with me. I was angry and resentful. We argued all the time about how much he was letting me down.

He just didn't know anything about how to treat a woman, and I had to lecture him constantly about what he was doing wrong. I just wanted to be treated right. He told me to stop trying to make him feel guilty and got really angry when we fought. Then he wouldn't talk to me for hours. I felt sad and lonely, but I wasn't going to back down. If he couldn't hear it my way, then he didn't appreciate how smart I was and didn't deserve me.

Now write two or three of your own scenarios in your journal. Look for your partner's attempts to tell you something that you didn't agree with and how you responded. Don't judge yourself or rationalize your behavior.

Did the arguments remind you of anything you witnessed or experienced as a child? Who played the role you play now? What was that person's status in your family? Did you want to emulate that person?

Step Two: Finding the Taproots of Your Need-to-Win Behavior

The compulsive need to win an argument is taught in childhood. Though children respond differently to challenges, they will learn to be competitive if the stakes are high enough. Exaggerated rewards or terrible punishments can spur any child to engage in combat. Arguments can be won with charm, anger, righteousness, threats, or guilt. They can be governed by rules that are fair, or dismissed in moot courts of preordained victors. The winners can be gracious and compassionate or arrogant and derisive.

What kind of winning behaviors did you observe as a child? What rewards did the winners receive, and what penalties were the losers obligated to endure?

EXERCISE: Winners and Losers

Make two lists in your journal. In the first list, put down all the positive and negative characteristics that were used to describe those people who won arguments when you were a child. In the second list, do the same for those who were the designated losers. For example, you might describe the argument winners as powerful, smart, resilient, tenacious, bullying, direct, mean, self-serving, and so on. You might describe the argument losers as weak, vulnerable, incompetent, unaware, easy to control, slow, rebellious, dumb, and so forth.

When you have finished making the two lists in your journal, ask yourself which characteristics best describe you when you argue with your adult partners. How do you feel about such labels or behaviors?

EXERCISE: The Rules for Winning

You are consciously or unconsciously operating from a set of combat assumptions that you learned when you were young. For you to reevaluate whether you still want to be living by those rules, you'll need to first identify them. Here are some examples:

"I must never show vulnerability."

"If my partner wins an argument, I'll feel stupid."

"I'll be responsible if my partner makes a wrong decision."

"I don't trust weakness in other people."

"I expect to win if I'm right."

"You can't trust other people to know what they are talking about."

"I am usually the winner in any argument because I'm right."

Write down your own winning practices. Compare them to those that were the house rituals in your family of origin. In what ways are they the same? Did you believe the house rituals in your family of origin were fair? Have you chosen to repeat them, or are you unconsciously following what you were taught? How have these practices affected your relationships?

Now that you have a better understanding of the origins of your need-to-win behavior, you are ready for the next step.

Step Three: Identifying the Triggers of Your Need-to-Win Behavior

If you hate to lose an argument and are righteous about being a winner, you will experience any perceived verbal challenge as a trigger to fight. If you have picked partners who will engage you until you win, your relationships will become more contentious over time. As the scorecard fills up, your closeness to your partner will diminish. Eventually, the battles will happen more often and the healing will take longer.

Once an argument starts, you may have difficulty stopping the intensity of your reaction. You've been programmed to respond quickly and effectively to maintain your advantage. If you want to change your behavior, you'll have to learn to slow down that automatic confrontation. By becoming less reactive, you'll be able to both see the argument coming and have an alternative behavior ready.

APPROACHING THE STARTING LINE

The following factors can determine your responses to confrontation:

The type of partner you choose: You're likely to be most attracted to people who remind you of the person who taught you to fight when you were a child or, alternatively, to those who remind you of the losers. Having internalized the battles you witnessed, you can play either role as an adult. The key to change is to identify and challenge the deeply entrenched patterns you learned in childhood and have alternative behaviors ready to substitute.

The gains or losses at stake: As a child in a need-to-win family, you gained or lost rewards according to how well you were able to argue. Your status with your family members was most likely evaluated by how well you were able to best your opponents. The more your partner resembles someone from your childhood, the more those same patterns will emerge and trigger you to win to preserve your reputation. Being aware of how the present can trigger the past can help you slow down your automatic responses.

How the rest of your life is going: If you are naturally susceptible to stress, or if the pressures in your life are at maximum level, you may be more easily seduced into a familiar fight just to relieve the tension. Being mindful of your current stress level will help you know when you're more likely to go off.

Your judgments about what your partner is saying: Having strong negative biases, intense prejudices, or strong dislikes will bring out your compulsive need to win if your partner disagrees with you. It's not wrong to feel deeply about whatever is your passion, but mixing it with a need to win can be deadly to a relationship.

If you can be aware of where you are, in terms of these different factors, you will be better able to avoid destructive confrontations.

Step Four: Examining When You Are Most Susceptible to Needing to Win

Your response to the statements in the next exercise will show your current need-to-win susceptibility.

EXERCISE: How Close Are Your Triggers to the Surface?

Rate the following statements of susceptibility on a scale of 1 to 5, where 1 = never, 2 = sometimes, 3 = usually, 4 = more often than not, and 5 = most of the time.

1. When you feel challenged, you can't stop until you win the argument.

2. Your partner reminds you of someone from your childhood.

3. You test your partner to see if he or she will try to win.

4. You get restless and bored if you can't get your partner to fight with you.

5. You're very reactive to your partner's approval.

6. You feel insecure after the fights are over.

7. You feel irritable and overstressed.

8. You fight with other people besides your partner.

9. You feel as if you're under a lot of pressure.

10. You're not getting the nurturing you need.

11. You disagree with your partner's ideas.

12. Your partner says things you dislike.

Now add up your score. If your score is under 30, you probably can keep yourself from reacting when your partner says something that sets you off. If it's 30 to 50, you'll need to be careful. If it's over 50, you're right on the edge and unlikely to keep from starting an argument. If you feel so easily reactive, it would be better to let things go for a while until you are less volatile.

You can use this set of questions whenever you want to check in with your need-to-win susceptibility. The next step is to seek a new vision as an alternative to needing to win all the time.

Step Five: Finding Alternatives to Needing to Win

Being competitive is so much a part of who you are that your new vision of yourself must include the strengths you have acquired from your battles. Otherwise, you will feel too vulnerable. Whether it's your challenging nature, your childhood modeling, or your fear of losing, you have honed your skills to triumph in battle. It would be unfair to ask you to leave the positives of those capabilities behind. But, because aspects of those same qualities alienate your partners, you will need to present them in a more effective way. The next two exercises will help.

EXERCISE: Your Battle Strengths

In your journal, make a list of those competitive qualities you respect and want to preserve when you leave the negatives of your need-to-win behavior behind. You can start with the positive adjectives you used in the first exercise in step two and add any others that come to mind.

Next, describe how you have typically used each of these qualities when interacting with your partners, and include what your partners have liked or disliked about these qualities when you used them to win arguments. Here are two examples:

1. "Directness: When I disagree with a partner, I am blunt and direct. My partners usually like the honesty that comes with my blunt statements. They also have told me that they feel uncomfortable when I seem insensitive to how my directness makes them feel."

2. "Confidence: When I express strong confidence in my opinion, my partners usually respect what I have to say. My partners have sometimes seen my confidence as arrogance, and told me that I seemed closed off and don't listen to what they have to say."

After you have finished with your examples, make a separate list with your competitive qualities and your partners' responses side by side. Use only the key words:

Direct = Insensitive

Confidence = Closed off

After you have finished your second list, you are ready to move on to the next exercise.

EXERCISE: Transforming the Negative into Positives

Talk with your partner honestly about your commitment to change your need-to-win behavior, and ask for your partner's point of view. Encouraged by your willingness to listen, your partner may understand how to help you keep the positive parts of your winning behavior while eliminating the negatives. Here are three different ways you can approach your partner to make that winning connection more possible:

1. Begin your statement with an honest explanation of why you behave the way you do, and say that you're concerned about your partner's feelings: "I know that I'm often blunt and direct, but I want to be open and honest with you. If I'm too insensitive, please let me know."

2. Phrase your winning quality as a question: "Am I being too direct with you?"

3. Anticipate what your partner may be feeling, and empathize: "I can see you pulling back, and you seem a little angry. I bet it's because my remark was pretty blunt." Or, "You're looking uncomfortable. It's probably because I tend to talk as if I'm the only expert here. That must be irritating."

If you are sincere in your desire to keep your positive winning qualities without having them result in destructive battles, these approaches will keep your partner in the game. You may feel awkward and a little vulnerable when you first practice this new behavior. But in the long run, you will reap the benefits of staying a winner without making your partner a loser.

Step Six: Finding Witnesses and Support for Connection Over Winning

Practice your new behavior whenever you have an opportunity and with anyone who will help you. Compulsive winning is a hard behavior to change and easily triggered. You must stay aware at all times of your level of reactivity, and either back away from destructive confrontations or make sure that whoever is helping you is informed of where you stand and what your goals are.

Past or current partners may be too angry or turned off to be objective witnesses to your new commitment. Or they themselves may be arguers, and have used counter-sabotage to activate your own compulsive-winning behaviors.

Any friends, past partners, or business colleagues who still see you as valuable despite your argumentative nature should be glad to work with you. They will welcome the opportunity to help and to interact in a new, more collaborative way. You'll need to give them permission to point out when you are revving up, and also be ready to back down and listen when they want to give you relevant feedback.

Step Seven: Staying Focused

Needing to win is a self-reinforcing relationship behavior. The more you do it, the more you are likely to do it again. The thirst for winning is a powerful aphrodisiac. To stay committed to seeking emotional and physical connection over winning, you'll need to have alternative behaviors clearly in mind.

EXERCISE: Your When-Instead Chart

In your journal write up to ten *when-instead statements* that are particularly relevant to your own trigger reactions. Here are some examples:

"*When* I feel the need to argue, I will *instead* listen more intently and ask for more information before I respond."

"*When* I feel the urge to prove my superior knowledge, I will *instead* try to appreciate what I can learn."

"*When* I feel like pushing my partner to hear and respect my opinion, I will *instead* ask if he or she is interested before I offer it."

"*When* I feel entitled to be supported in my point of view, I will *instead* be appreciative when my partner validates me."

"*When* I'm frightened of being erased and want to run away, I will *instead* tell my partner and ask for support."

"When I feel judgmental of my partner's opinions, I will *instead* try to understand him or her more deeply and open my mind and heart to new possibilities."

These are only a few examples. Go over your journal notes and create your own when-instead list to keep from slipping into your old patterns.

Keep this list somewhere where you can see it every day. As new alternatives arise, add them to the list. After a while, you will find yourself hearing these statements in your mind in real time and look forward to catching yourself in time to turn your behavior around.

7

Pessimism:
"If You Don't Expect Anything, You Won't Be Disappointed"

Pessimists believe that the blessings in life will always be outweighed by the costs. They worry that negative consequences will result from their actions, and fear they will be unable to cope when they do. "Nothing ventured, nothing gained" becomes "nothing ventured, nothing lost." Certain that trust in the future can bring only disappointment, they see their world through a prism of suspicion, mistrust, and doubt. To maintain their protective walls, they discount hope, minimize joy, and discredit possibilities.

Living with the cup always half empty, pessimists suffer from a feeling of helplessness and fear of the future. Efforts to cheer them up are often responded to with "yes, but" or "you just don't understand" or a silent wry smile and pained, rolling eyes. Somewhere in that gloom seems to be an idealist gone down, who desperately wants to believe in possibilities but cannot risk more disillusionment.

PESSIMISM IS LEARNED

Children are not born with a negative attitude. They can be genetically susceptible to depression and anxiety, more sensitive to disapproval, or less resilient, but mistrust is a learned response. Even the most innately optimistic child can be taught to expect disillusionment when life's challenges hurt too much and healing is in short supply. Broken promises, irrational punishment, emotional and physical deprivation or abuse, multiple losses, the inability to gain what's needed, or crushed hopes can form the foundation of learned pessimism.

A skeptical and mistrusting view of the future is often passed down through generations and cultures and taught as a respected tradition. Better to be prepared against the probabilities of loss than be caught unawares:

"We face reality."

"No one in this family is ever taken for a fool."

"Don't count your chickens before they hatch."

"Everything's a deal, baby. You don't get something for nothing."

"Don't expect someone to catch you every time you fall."

Such inherited mistrustful outlooks can be difficult to leave behind. Pessimists often feel certain that if they are more optimistic and trusting, they will be open to exploitation. A selective attention to negative consequences supports their deeply held beliefs.

MISTRUST IN RELATIONSHIPS

If you have been a pessimistic relationship saboteur and continue to practice negativity in your relationships, you may unconsciously be searching for the one person who can inspire you to hope again. That desire may have attracted many optimistic cheerleaders who have tried to win your trust, but you most probably have outlasted their attempts to point out the positives of life. Enough resistance will contaminate positive energy over time, and the results of continued pessimism will wear out the most dedicated of rescuers.

By now, you may realize how many positive people you have attracted and defeated, wondering how things might have been had you let go of your pessimistic outlook. If you are ready to leave your negativity behind, your life and your relationships will change in ways you have never dreamed possible.

THE SEVEN STEPS TO RECOVERY

Negativity is fully healable, but the demons of pessimism are strong. They have driven you to repeatedly dwell on negative events and use the past to anticipate the future. To change your focus, you don't have to pretend that troubles do not exist. But you do have to replace the expectation of doom with a more realistic expectation of hope.

Step One: Observing Your Pessimistic Patterns Without Judgment

If many partners have left you because of your pessimistic attitude, they probably gave up after trying and failing to make you feel more hopeful. Unfortunately, their leaving you has further reinforced your negative expectations. Your pessimism may have protected you from disappointment, but it has also kept you from trust, intimacy, and sustained love.

To understand how you have behaved in relationships, you'll need to reexamine some of your negative responses. Do not allow yourself to become negative in the process. This is the time to simply observe without any self-judgment.

EXERCISE: Contrasting Negative and Positive Beliefs

Your first exercise is to create a fantasy dialogue between you and an imaginary optimistic partner. In your journal, write a series of brief dialogues between yourself and that partner, in which you voice your negative opinions and your imaginary partner responds with his or her optimistic ones. Here's an example:

You:	You should always be ready to lose everything, so you won't feel sad when you do.
Your imagined partner:	Live your life fully until whatever losses occur.

You:	Nothing ever works out, so why believe it will? You'll just get hurt.
Your imagined partner:	I usually learn something important from every experience in my life. Otherwise, I wouldn't be the person I am. I don't want to live my life in regret or have my losses predict my future.
You:	When you open your heart, you just get hurt. I'd rather be alone than risk that again.
Your imagined partner:	I know I can get hurt when I love deeply, but it's worth it.
You:	It's better to expect the worst; then you won't be disappointed.
Your imagined partner:	I think disappointments happen. I'm not going to let that stop me from searching for the great outcomes.

The goal of this exercise is for you to observe the contrast between your negativity and your partner's optimism. When you have completed your own list, answer the following questions in your journal:

1. If your statements are true, are your partner's untrue?

2. Where did you learn what you believe?

3. Why do you resist looking at your life in a more positive way?

4. Have your doubts and skepticism blocked your openness to other alternatives?

5. What would actually happen if you were to let go of some of your beliefs?

6. Can you look at your negative behavior and have compassion for yourself when you think about how you became this way?

After doing this exercise, are you better able to understand what drives you to continue your pessimistic beliefs? Can you begin to see where they came from?

Step Two: Finding the Taproots of Your Pessimism

There is usually at least one significant person in a family who destroys the hope that children seek. That person can be the carrier of generational pessimism or someone who is suffering from his or her own personal losses and cannot trust the future. By modeling or by direct interaction, this person sows the seeds of despair. Those pessimistic beliefs take hold very early in life, grow with each negative outcome, and are impervious to joy. They can be learned through many experiences:

- repeatedly broken promises

- unexpected and irrational punishments

- anticipated losses or exaggeration of potential disappointments

- immobilization and helplessness in the face of challenge

- no opportunities for satisfaction of needs

- repeatedly undermined hopes for change

- mocked optimism

- pride in seeing and preparing for negative outcomes

EXERCISE: Remembering Past Negative Dialogues

Pick two or three experiences from the preceding list that bring up childhood memories. For each one, recall a scene, remembering where you were and who demonstrated pessimism to you. Write what you remember in detail, paying close attention to your feelings. If you can, create an imaginary dialogue with this person. Here's an example of the experience of repeatedly undermined hope for change:

I'm about eight years old, sitting with my maternal grandmother. She is from the old country and very set in her ways. I love her stories and her wisdom, but I never like the endings. Everyone in the stories learns important lessons, but they never get what they want. There is no hope for change, but the people are respected for tolerating injustice and surviving their martyrdom. I want the people to get what they want, so I try to change the endings, but my grandmother scolds me for not facing the truth and for being disrespectful.

Me: Nana, why can't these people do something that will help them?

Nana: They don't have any options.

Me: People can always try something else.

Nana: You are very naïve. Not everyone in this world can have what they want. Maybe you have too much.

Me: I just want them to be happy.

Nana: Not everyone is happy. You are expecting things that are not part of the real world.

Me: Are you happy, Nana?

Nana: I accept my life the way it is, and I don't complain.

When you have finished writing, can you better understand where your pessimistic viewpoints may have originated? Can you see how your hopes and dreams were continually undermined? Have you carried those patterns into your present life?

Step Three: Identifying What Triggers Your Pessimistic Behavior

Triggers are events, people, or situations that activate your pessimism. You must identify what those personal triggers are, so you can be aware of your reaction in time to change it.

Your triggers can be anything that reminds you of unavoidable loss as a child. Recent failures can also activate those early memories. In your current relationship, your pessimistic behavior can be triggered even when your partner attempts to cheer you up when you feel down or discouraged, or doubt the outcome of the relationship.

If your partner tries to make you feel more hopeful, do you respond with any of the following resistance barriers?

"I've already tried that. I know it won't work."

"I'm just too upset to do anything right now."

"You just don't understand. If you did, you would see that I can't fix this."

"Stop trying to make things seem better than they are. If I'm unhappy, there's a good reason."

"It may be easy for you, but I'm not you."

"Your suggestions are unrealistic."

"Everything in the world can't be solved just because you want it to."

"There is nothing good about this situation. Don't try to make it better than it is."

"If I'm pulling you down, just leave me alone. I'm better off by myself when I'm like this."

EXERCISE: What Do You Say When Your Partner Tries to Help?

Think about how you respond when your partner tries to make you feel better. Write these responses in your journal. If they are accompanied by any feelings, write the feelings next to the statements. Look at them briefly each evening so that you will be more aware of your typical responses.

Remember, your partner can only last so long on the receiving end of your pessimism. You might ask your partner how he or she feels when you continually resist attempts to alleviate your negativity.

EXERCISE: Becoming Your Own Positive Partner

In the exercise in step one, where you imagined a partner's positive responses, you could see how negative your automatic responses have been. Now, make yourself your own partner. Try to remember as many negative statements as you can that you have made to yourself or to your partners, and replace them with positive counter responses. The more exaggerated your responses, the better. You may even begin to see some humor in these changes. Hopefully, after several examples, you'll be able to more clearly see the barriers you have put up for others and be eager to bring them down:

Pessimistic statement: I'm just too upset to do anything right now.

Alternative: There are so many incredible, happy, satisfying, pleasurable, and healing things I could do to feel better.

Pessimistic statement: I don't want to be fixed. If I'm unhappy, there's a good reason, and I should be able to be miserable if that's truly the way I feel.

Alternative: I am absolutely sick and tired of being unhappy. I not only want to be fixed, I want to feel glorious and positive. I'm ready and willing to look at any alternative that will help me feel better.

The more you can create new examples, the better. As you do this exercise, you may experience feelings of resistance and rebellion. Those pessimistic responses reflect your unconscious loyalty to the people who taught you how to feel that way. You may also feel anxiety about giving up the feelings that have protected you from the disappointment of loss. Have faith. These feelings will decrease as you realize how unhappy those people were.

Step Four: Examining When You Are Most Susceptible to Pessimism

Negative feelings activate depression, which can cloud your ability to see beyond them. Depression can, in turn, increase your negative feelings, especially if your depression is the result of a biochemical imbalance. A current significant loss will add to your heaviness. Illness, loss of your support network, and being down in resources can reinforce pessimistic beliefs. Pessimism can, unfortunately, be a comfort if your life is out of control and you don't think you deserve better.

Taking better care of yourself can reduce your pessimistic responses. Exercise, good sleep, and staying away from roller-coaster foods like caffeine, alcohol, and refined sugars can make a huge difference in a short time. Hanging around positive people can help also, unless they activate your rebellious need to invalidate them.

Whatever disappointments you may be experiencing right now, you need to remember that they are not everything. What is true now may not be true later, and you may not see all the options. You can free yourself to see alternative perspectives.

Without realizing it, many pessimistic people do use positive coping mechanisms, even if they are not aware of them. Children naturally move toward pleasure and away from pain. If most of their hopes are dashed, they will still cling to those hopes that they can. As adults, they may act superstitiously, fearing that if they hope something will happen, it will be less likely to happen. But, deep inside, they don't let their losses take away all pleasure, even if they continue to deny that good things will happen.

For you to leave your pessimistic behavior behind, you'll need to uncover and recognize those coping mechanisms that exist under the surface. They will be crucial components of your transformation.

EXERCISE: Finding Your Hidden Coping Mechanisms

In your journal, list some different ways you have pulled yourself out of pessimistic spirals in the past. Then, on a scale of 1 to 4, where 1 = not at all, 2 = occasionally, 3 = often, and 4 = most of the time, rate how often you are using each of your coping mechanisms. If you like, you can customize the following list of coping mechanisms to make them reflect your own.

Example: Whenever you feel negative and pessimistic about the future, you have learned to:

1. Take care of yourself physically.

2. Pursue your spirituality.

3. Divert yourself by doing something kind for someone else.

4. Search for perspective to help you see how you have exaggerated your situation.

5. Call a good friend who will let you vent and not try to change the way you feel.

6. Take some time away from everyone and reprioritize what's truly important.

7. Remember what you love about your life.

8. Think about how to find more satisfaction.

9. Ask your partner for nurturing.

The goal here is to see that your pessimism doesn't control all of you, all of the time. Check in every week with how you're coping. Rate yourself again on how often you use your coping mechanisms. Any given score is not as important as its upward direction. If you develop new positive coping mechanisms, add them to your list.

Step Five: Learning How to Leave Your Pessimism Behind

Inside many pessimistic people are idealists who want to believe in happiness. Your negative attitude has caused you grief in your relationships, but it has also protected you. Letting it go will leave you unarmored until you are secure in your commitment to leave your pessimism behind.

To stay fortified as you change, you must recognize the times in your life when your fear of loss has not stopped you from being courageous. These moments were not accidental. Careful not to minimize their importance. Try to remember and list your own courageous acts. Give them the same respect you would those of someone you loved deeply.

EXERCISE: Your Courageous Acts

In your journal, write about three or more times in your life when you did not allow your pessimism to get in the way of what you wanted. Note what you did to overcome your negative tendencies and push forward despite them. Here's an example:

I remember wanting to try out for the tennis team in high school. I knew I wasn't good enough because I'd played with some of the other players before and they were much better. I played out the scenario in my head a hundred times, trying to work out how I'd leave the field when I lost. It would be easier to expect nothing than to deal with the grief of not making the team, but somehow I just felt I had to try.

The coach looked surprised when I showed up, but I was determined not to show him my fear. I thought about my best friend, who had lost a leg to cancer when he was three. I tried to remember what my grandpa told me about never giving up. I read somewhere that you can overcome anxiety by turning it into power. When I finally got on the court, I put my worry aside and just played my best, and I made the team. I could hardly believe it. It felt wonderful.

Writing about your successes will remind you of those times when you used courage to override your pessimism. A certainty that things will never work out is a superstitious belief, taught to you when you were young. You've been programmed to expect the worst and to minimize anything positive that may have happened instead. How were you able to put those teachings aside when you faced uncertainty with courage instead of defeat?

From now on, until you feel confident that your courage will hold, pay attention to the times you practiced courage when you expected a bad outcome. If you're discouraged, remind yourself of the times when you did not let pessimism stop you.

Step Six: Finding Witnesses and Support for Your New Outlook

This will be your most difficult step. You have been a pessimistic relationship saboteur who has worn down your partners by invalidating their optimism and reinforcing your negativity in the process. You have become a skilled warrior in defeating your opponents. Now you'll need to intentionally open your heart to people who can help you believe in possibilities.

The people you pick must be able to objectively witness your new commitments without feeling sorry for you or trying to fix you. They will need to understand that your distress is not their responsibility, even when you have difficulty holding on to your new outlook.

Pessimistic people have a multitude of appealing facial expressions and voice intonations that can lure people into feeling sorry for them. Therefore, you may want to communicate with your witnesses mostly in writing. Try instant messaging or e-mail.

If you are currently in a long-term relationship, your partner may be unable to resist encouraging, supporting, and validating you each time you make a little headway. Ask your partner to avoid doing that. You need to feel your own triumph when you fight your negativity. Rather than help, his or her exaggerated responses could activate your mistrust and push you back into despondency.

Step Seven: Staying Focused

Living in apprehension of doom can feel like a yoke around your neck. As you practice your new behaviors, that burden will slowly lift. The lightness of being that follows will become your most potent reason for staying on your new path. It takes time to get there. In the meantime, you are bound to feel frightened and vulnerable as you begin to take more risks.

You can fight your fears by exaggerating and contrasting them to a more logical reality. If you look at the past, you will most likely see that most of what you feared would happen did not come to pass.

EXERCISE: Contrasting Your Expectations with Reality

At the beginning of each day, think about the challenges you face, and purposefully expect them to result in the most dire consequences you can imagine. Be as mistrusting and pessimistic as you can possibly be. In your journal, list at least five things you are going to do that day and write down the most terrible thing that could happen in each case. Here's an example:

> *I have to speak at an important meeting today. I'm going to sound totally stupid, my suit will be inappropriate, and the other members of my committee will wonder why they even asked me to join. I'll*

spill coffee on the new conference room rug, and my boss will walk by just as I flub the presentation.

After you have listed five expectations for the day, put your journal aside and live your day practicing the new optimism you've learned. When you come back in the evening, write down what actually happened during the day rather than what you anticipated:

I was totally prepared. My presentation went better than expected. I was nervous, but so was everyone else, and they didn't seem to care. I even made them laugh in a couple of places. I heard later that word got back to my boss, and he was excited about my contribution. Perhaps it wasn't my best, but it was certainly much better than I had anticipated.

You'll see some powerful contrasts between the expectations of a pessimist and the realistic predictions of a person who faces the future as the adventure it should be.

EXERCISE: Accepting Compliments

The last part of your transformation will be to learn how to accept encouragement and compliments without believing they are just manipulations or potential exploitations. You probably have dismissed so many supportive feelings in your past relationships that learning to differentiate what's well intended from what's potentially manipulative will take some time.

This is where your current partner can be a blessing. Tell your partner that you need to take your doubting seriously, but you don't want it to erase what someone sincerely offers. If your partner compliments you, perhaps you can politely ask your partner to tell you more about what motivated him or her to do so. Tell your partner that you may initially deflect anything positive but you're trying to be more positive. You are understandably uncomfortable letting yourself want something that may never happen. Ask for patience and understanding.

At the end of each day, write down in your journal any compliments you received that day. Then write down how you might have received them before and what you are trying to do differently now. It may take you several months to trust your own responses and to start returning support and encouragement to others, but it will happen.

Remember, your pessimism is a learned response. You were taught that gullibility and unbridled optimism might leave you unprepared for life's catastrophes. Only a devotion to pessimism could protect you. Hopefully, you've seen that it has done the opposite and you are now free to live in life's possibilities rather than in its potential tragedies.

Needing to Be Center Stage: "Pay Attention to Me"

Center-stage relationship saboteurs seek the attention of the people around them, and they feel disconnected and uninterested when they can't get that attention. Even when they realize that being attentive to others would be to their advantage, they seem unable to relinquish the spotlight.

If center-stage people happen to be famous or charismatic, they may enjoy an endless array of adoring audiences. But, if they lack those assets, they may command the attention they covet by being insistent and demanding, intimidating others into polite acquiescence. In all cases, center-stage people end up holding their audiences hostage to their own self-absorption.

The origins of this behavior are not always obvious. In some cases, center-stage people may have been those adored children who loved to perform and had appreciative family audiences. But, more often, the early life experiences of center-stage people did not provide them with guaranteed emotional sustenance. They more probably had to fight for the attention they needed, and still believe that commanding the attention of others is the only sure way to get it.

Whatever their reasons, center-stage relationship saboteurs end up exploiting others by demanding disproportionate amounts of time and attention. They cannot stay quiet before a potential audience, whether that audience is of many people or just one. Seemingly insatiable, they leave no room for the opinions or needs of others.

If you think you consistently monopolize conversations, drown others out, or keep returning the attention to yourself, you may be a center-stage saboteur. Center-stage behavior and true intimacy are strangers. To enjoy genuine connection with others, you'll need to learn to share the stage without feeling resentful or devalued.

WHY YOU MAY SEEK TO BE CENTER STAGE

Below is a list of some reasons why you may choose to take center stage despite the intimacy you are sacrificing in the process:

- As a child, you were rewarded with approval for entertaining your family.

- Members of your family lived vicariously through you.

- You become anxious with silences in conversation and need to fill them.

- You're afraid that you won't be noticed unless you take center stage.

- In your family, the most entertaining person got the most attention.

- Others have often told you that gatherings are never the same without you.

- You believe that your contributions are more valuable than those of others.

- Social situations make you nervous, and you can't stay quiet.

- You cannot sense what others are feeling, and are insecure if you don't take charge.

- You take responsibility for keeping social interactions interesting.

- You're searching for your verbal soul mate, the one person who can keep up with you.

- You need nurturing and attention, and don't know any other way to get it.

- You were the child of a narcissistic parent, and have absorbed his or her ways.

Do any of these reasons apply to you? If so, make a list of them, adding any others that come to mind. Keep this list in your journal for later reference.

BEHIND THE SPOTLIGHT

The inner world of most center-stage relationship saboteurs is not one of conceit or comfort. When alone, some relive their social interactions with remorse and embarrassment. Others struggle to rationalize their behavior, trying to convince themselves that their one-person show was appreciated and necessary. Those with real or imagined status may believe that their center-stage behavior was a gift to everyone.

If your center-stage behavior has lost you intimate connections with the people you love, you can take heart. Boredom, silence, and anxiety are not your only other options. There are other ways of being that will support your own needs but allow for the needs of others as well.

THE SEVEN STEPS TO RECOVERY

Your first step in your transformation will be to understand the origins of your center-stage behavior and how you express it in your adult relationships.

Step One: Observing Your Center-Stage Behavior Without Judgment

This first step will be the hardest. If you have practiced center-stage behavior all your life, you won't be able to easily observe yourself from the outside or pay attention to your partner's responses. The good news is that once you have conquered this step, later steps will be much easier for you to master.

In the following exercise, collect as much data about your behavior as you can without allowing negative self-criticism to cloud your vision. Your goal will be to understand what others around you have been feeling while they have watched you perform. Pretend that you are a disinterested camera, simply watching yourself and photographing the situation.

EXERCISE: Capturing the Invisible Dialogue

Recall a situation with a partner where you monopolized the conversation. Write about the scenario in your journal, answering the following questions: Where were you? What was the occasion? Was this a relatively new partner, or were you in an established relationship? Can you evaluate the level of emotional closeness you both felt at the time? How did your partner react when you began to take center stage? What was your response?

After setting the scene, try to re-create both the spoken dialogue between yourself and your partner, and what each of you may have thought but not said. Do your best to imagine what must have been in your partner's head. Here's an example:

> *My boyfriend and I were in a restaurant having dinner. We were there to celebrate the third anniversary of our first date. I think I felt more expectations of the evening than he did. He wasn't saying much and seemed a little distant. I felt insecure and anxious that something was going on because he's told me how much he hates it when I start performing. I tried to stay quiet, but it was really hard. I didn't want the evening to be boring, and felt I was the only one who could make something exciting happen.*

Me: Anything going on? You seem so quiet.

Partner: No, just tired.

Me: (*Getting anxious. Starting to feel insecure. Feeling a little discounted. Watching his face for signs of trouble. Feel like I'd better fill in the space.*) I went out to lunch today with my boss. He assured me that I was going to get the new job. Do you think it's a good idea? I've asked other people, and they're not sure I'm making the right move. They think maybe he's going to make a pass at me. I've had situations like this before and didn't see them coming, so I don't want to be stupid. What do you think, honey?

Partner: *(Thinking: I was hoping we could just have a nice, quiet dinner. She always has some crisis going on. I'm sure I'm in for an hour-long monologue. She's a great girl, but she can't seem to stop talking. Maybe if I stay quiet, it won't last as long.)* Sounds like you need more information.

Me: *(Thinking: I see that he's not listening very well, but I really need attention right now. I just need to tell him a little more about it. Maybe he'll get more interested as time goes on.)* I'm really worried, and I can't seem to stop thinking about it. I need your input. You know my boss and how he operates. I heard a rumor that he did it to someone else. I've checked it out on the Internet, and the information is frightfully conflicting.

Partner: Okay. *(Thinking: She's not going to stop until she gets all this out. Sounds like a long night. I don't know why she doesn't get that I'm not that interested. I don't want to hurt her, though, especially on our anniversary. I'll try to hear her out.)*

In this scenario, the center-stage person is anxious and fearful of losing the attention she needs. She isn't able to read beyond what her partner is saying and isn't in touch with how he feels. Your scenario may be very different, but the goal is the same: to listen to your own inner dialogue and imagine what your partner is thinking but not saying.

Just being aware of your behavior and its effect on others can motivate you to want to change. You may want to refer back to your personal reasons for taking center stage to look for further clues to help with your transformation.

Step Two: Finding the Taproots of Your Center-Stage Behavior

Young children naturally want to command center stage. If they continue to demand undue attention, they are often rebuffed. As they grow and develop, they learn to share the spotlight with others because it brings more social success. Through experience, they learn to repress their inappropriate need for attention in favor of acceptance and positive feedback.

Adults who continue to demand center stage despite the unfavorable reactions of others have somehow failed to learn appropriate boundaries. Whether such negative patterns have been learned by programming, modeling, or trauma, they are unconscious barriers to transforming. Even when challenged by loving or frustrated partners, center-stage adults may find themselves unable to stop what they are doing. When confronted, they may try to excuse their behavior:

I was raised in a family with eight children and two working parents. Man, if you wanted to be heard, you knocked everyone out of the way for a few moments in the limelight. Once you had it, you better not let it go because you'd never know if it would happen again. You'll just have to forgive me if I hog the plate. I can't be any other way.

Or they may say:

My dad traveled all the time. When he was home, I wanted all his attention. I learned to do all the things he liked to keep him focused on me. I never got enough. When I love someone, I need that focus or I start to feel the same terrible sadness I felt when he would leave again. Whoever wants to be in a relationship with me just can't take it personally.

Your justifications for becoming a center-stage person will always be legitimate for you, but holding on to that behavior will never get you the authentic attention and love you crave. Understanding the roots of your center-stage behavior and learning better options will help you believe that love will more likely come your way when you stop demanding it. Once you realize that you can still get the attention you need without paying such a heavy price, you can look forward to the future instead of holding on to the past.

THE NARCISSISTIC PARENT

One of the most pervasive causes of center-stage behavior is having a narcissistic parent. If a narcissistic parent is the primary caregiver, a child may develop reactive self-preserving behavior. The child's center-stage behavior comes from continually needing to establish the right to be validated by a parent who cannot emotionally make room for him or her. Giving up center stage as an adult activates childhood terrors of being emotionally erased. If this describes your situation, you will need to understand how your narcissistic parent's behavior has affected you.

Narcissistic people see the world through their own egocentricity. People in their lives are often reduced to objects that either fulfill or block their desires. Narcissists are consumed with their own self-importance and inflated sense of self-worth. They feel entitled to automatic admiration and respect, whatever they do. Their expectations must be anticipated and met, regardless of the feelings of others. They cannot feel what someone else is experiencing and do not consider that the needs of others are as important as their own.

These are the beliefs of a narcissistic person:

- "I am more important than you."

- "I am so special, you must accept anything I do or say as right."

- "Your value is dependent upon making me feel essential and esteemed."

- "Your job is to make me feel important."

- "You should fulfill my needs without complaining."

- "You should always put my needs above yours."

- "I am entitled to things that you aren't entitled to."

- "No one will ever be as wonderful as I am."

If this list of entitlements reminds you of a parent or other significant person in your childhood, you may have unconsciously internalized those entitlements as an alternative to bending under the will of a narcissist; the following exercise will help you. If you believe that your center-stage behavior comes from other sources, you can skip to the next section.

EXERCISE: Did a Narcissistic Parent Raise You?

In your journal, write down the name of your narcissistic parent and how he or she expected you to believe and behave. Write down how you felt as a child on the receiving end of your parent's narcissistic behavior. Then, ask yourself if you internalized those parental expectations and have transferred them to others.

As you recall your experiences, you will understand how much you have continued to fear being erased again. That understanding will help you to stay in touch with your partner's feelings when you begin to express your parental behaviors toward him or her. For most narcissistically wounded children, this awareness is enough to help them conquer their center-stage behavior.

Step Three: Identifying What Triggers Your Center-Stage Behavior

Whatever your personal reasons are for becoming a center-stage saboteur, here are the most common triggers that activate center-stage behavior:

- Being with someone who either withholds attention or lavishes you with adulation.

- Suspecting that someone is uninterested in what you have to say.

- Needing nurturing and not knowing how else to get it.

- Feeling competitive with someone else who is better at getting the attention you need.

- Feeling bored with what's going on and needing to fix it.

- Feeling anxious.

- Worrying that no one will like you if you don't entertain.

- Feeling left out and unimportant.

To change your center-stage behavior, you'll need to understand when you feel triggered and be prepared to act differently. The best way is to recall your earliest memories of when you either took center stage or were on the receiving end of this kind of behavior in your family.

EXERCISE: Watching the Show

As if you were an outside observer, reenter a moment in your childhood when you or someone else was the center of attention. In your journal, describe the scene in as much detail as possible. Answer the following questions: What preceded the center-stage behavior? Who was present? What role did you play? What were you feeling? Whether it was you or someone else, how did the people there react to the center-stage person? Here's an example:

> *I'm playing outside by myself. My mother asks me to come inside because my aunt and uncle are visiting. She's already told them I would do something, and they look as if they are anticipating a performance. I know my mother needs to show me off because she always does when other people visit. She plays the piano while I sing my kindergarten song. Everyone claps hard and tells me I'm wonderful. When I'm done, she tells me to go back outside. My importance to her is over for the time being. She won't pay attention to me again until it's important to her. She only cares about me when it benefits her.*

After you have written your own scenario, ask yourself these additional questions:

- Are you still seeking attention in the same way you did as a child?

- What part do you insist that your partners play?

- What do you feel and do when you get what you want?

- What happens when you don't get what you want?

Whether your center-stage behavior comes from modeling, indulgence, or trauma, you have probably not known the joy of attention that comes from neither performance nor demand. Learning to give up center-stage behavior may bring you a happiness you have never experienced before.

Step Four: Examining When You Are Most Susceptible to Center-Stage Behavior

Being less reactive to center-stage triggers can help you change your behavior in your current relationships. The best way to become less reactive is to expose your fear of being less important when you don't demand center stage.

EXERCISE: Exploring Your Fears

Rate the following statements of what you may fear on a scale of 1 to 5, where 1 = never, 2 = rarely, 3 = sometimes, 4 = usually, and 5 = always.

1. If you don't get the attention you need, you become afraid that your partner doesn't love you anymore.

2. When your partner lavishes attention on you, you think it's just a pretense.

3. When your partner seems uninterested in what you're saying, you think he's bored.

4. If you can't get the nurturing you want, you're probably not worth it.

5. If your partner acts as if someone else is more interesting than you are, you feel envious and competitive.

6. When you're not interested in what your partner is saying, you're afraid he will think you don't love him.

7. When things are dull between your partner and you, you think that your love is dying.

8. You get anxious when your partner doesn't seem to enjoy what you're saying or doing.

9. If you can't be center stage, you don't know what else to do.

Add up your score. If your score is under 20, you are not as frightened of losing center stage as you think you are. You have a good chance of changing your center-stage behavior by simply facing it. If your score is between 20 and 30, you are still somewhat owned by your fears. If your score is over 30, your triggers are set to go off. You are still at their mercy, and they have kept you monopolizing the attention in your relationships.

Come back to this exercise each month and answer these questions again to see if your fears are decreasing over time. You may also want to think about whether your answers as an adult closely reflect how you felt as a child. If they do, you will know that your fears today have strong taproots in your past.

Step Five: Learning How to Share the Stage

The most important two lessons a center-stage person must learn are how to share the spotlight and how to be a great audience to others. To do that, you need to practice giving others the same support, interest, and validation you have spent your life seeking.

Here are some simple guidelines for making sure you're sharing the spotlight with your partner:

1. Don't interrupt when your partner needs your attention.

2. Ask sincere questions.

3. Keep your advice and opinions to yourself unless asked.

4. Find a way to become interested in what your partner is saying.

5. Make your target your partner's comfort and satisfaction.

6. Generously give what you want to receive.

You'll notice that these are the expectations you've had of others. Now it's time to give back the attention you've demanded from others in the past. Every day, try to find at least one person with whom you can practice these simple guidelines as a good listener. Practice whenever you can, even if you're having a short conversation.

If you're currently in a relationship, go over these guidelines regularly with your partner. As your partner responds positively to your authentic desire to share the stage, you may find yourself enjoying the comfort of letting someone else be the performer. You may also find that you have more authentic attention than you've ever known.

EXERCISE: The Blessings of Being a Supporting Actor

Evaluate yourself on how well you can tolerate the background role. This exercise will set your intention before you allow yourself to seek the central role again. In your journal, rate these statements of intent on a scale of 1 to 4, where 1 = don't agree, 2 = sometimes agree, 3 = mostly agree, and 4 = always agree.

1. It feels good to let your partner be more important than you are.

2. It's right to share the stage with other people even if they aren't as entertaining as you are.

3. It's important to give people as much time as they need to express themselves.

4. Adoration is not love.

5. It's great to help other people shine, even if you're less important at that moment.

6. It's as good to be a great listener as it is to be the center of attention.

7. You want people to appreciate you because you help them appreciate themselves.

Add up your score. What it adds up to right now is less important than improving your score over time.

Do this exercise each week until your new behaviors become their own reward. Write down any feelings that arise as you repeat this exercise. They may help you better understand where your sabotaging behavior originated.

Step Six: Finding Witnesses and Support for Sharing the Stage

Just about everyone you know who is still around will gladly support you in your new efforts. The partners who couldn't tolerate your sabotaging behavior have probably disappeared, and your stalwart supporters have, no doubt, liked you despite your egocentricity. If your partner is excited about your new commitment, he or she can be a great support.

You'll need to be careful to avoid taking center stage as you tell others about how you are changing. Your challenge is to convince your friends, colleagues, and partners that your current motives aren't simply self-serving, as they may have been in the past. They may doubt you at first, but they will encourage your wish to change your behavior for others. They may also have some past resentments that they want to tell you about. Listen openly and thank them for their feedback. Those honest reflections may help you stay committed to your task. Here are some guidelines:

- Tell your friends what you're up to.

- Ask them for examples from the past.

- Monitor how much and when you speak, and make sure your audience is willingly listening.

- If someone else has the floor, practice your commitment to make them feel attended to.

- Ask for appropriate feedback on your progress.

Step Seven: Staying Focused

The first step on your road to recovery was the hardest, and this last one will be your second-most-difficult step. The strokes for performing are tempting, especially if you're good at it. With luck and effort, you will gain equal admiration for being a good audience for others.

EXERCISE: Monitoring Your Interactions

Each evening, take a few minutes to monitor your actions from earlier in the day. In your journal write down any interactions you had during the day where you had the opportunity to take center stage, whether you did so or not. Do not count activities like running a meeting at work, where you were supposed to be the leader. Thinking back to the events of the day, ask yourself when you brought the attention back to yourself and when you were able to give it away.

Do not negatively judge yourself if you cannot stay on track all the time. Instead, ask yourself how you were triggered and if you could have anticipated it. Emphasize the times you were able to make the right choice, and give yourself credit. With your new behavior, you may discover a more sincerely adoring audience. Combining your skills as a performer with your new vulnerable and open self could prove to be a great attraction.

9

Addictions:
"I've Got to Have That"

All human beings ponder the past and wonder about the future, searching for lessons and hoping their dreams will come true. But, if those twin contemplations stir feelings of remorse or anxiety, most people try to avoid them by finding a way to stay in the moment.

"But," the addict says, "what if the present moments are also filled with sadness, boredom, frustration, fear, or entrapment? What if there's no respite or place to feel at peace? What if the only escape is some mind-altering process that can make life feel beautiful again and temporarily erase those inescapable burdens?"

Addicts often rationalize their compulsive choices with these questions. They feel they must somehow escape the pressures that are too much for them to tolerate or else be doomed to a life without enough excitement or pleasure.

Whether driven by the need to avoid pain or the desire to enrich experience, addicts do not intend to harm themselves or others when they begin using. However, over time, their more innocuous urges become the cravings and obsessions that can destroy their relationships and sometimes their lives.

The cycle of addiction can be harsh. Chronic users of addictive escapes typically return from their escapes dissipated and guilty, rendering them less able to face the burdens left behind. Soon, both the cost of the addictive behavior and life without it become unbearable. The addict is enslaved and trapped, unable to live any part of life without shame and loss.

Addictive escapes can take many forms, but they share some common characteristics:

- They fuel obsessive thoughts and compulsive habits.

- They feel urgent.

- They seduce and demand continuous focus.

- They do not respond to rational arguments.

- They cost the addict emotionally, spiritually, physically, and financially.

- They redefine other responsibilities and relationships as unwanted interruptions.

- Unless healed, they gain strength over time.

- Their victims eventually blur the boundaries between integrity and immorality.

- Their users cycle through procuring, satiating, suffering, rationalizing, hungering, and using again.

- They destroy relationships over time.

Addicts were once thought of as self-indulgent, amoral people who took their pleasure at others' expense and had little remorse for their actions. Defined by their inability to put anything before their addictive hungers, they were automatically untrustworthy and disrespected sinners. If their addictions became chronic and deeply entrenched, they often lived up to their reputation, destroying friends, family, and self along the way. Programs designed to help them were often humiliating, intended to make the addict feel the pain he or she had irresponsibly inflicted on others.

Thankfully, addiction has become recognized as a disease. The causes are now understood to include underlying chemical imbalances, childhood modeling, unresolved trauma, social pressures, and the easy availability of negative outlets. Whether the target is alcohol, drugs, gambling, sex, food, work, shopping, video games, or the Internet, addiction is now seen as a life-destroying compulsion, and addicts are more often treated with understanding and support. Many people can now seek treatment without fear of the lifelong stigma that once was the price of exposure.

There are some addicts who are uninterested in becoming rehabilitated. They often live out their lives using others as vehicles to secure their habits or as barriers to be eliminated. But most addicts feel terrible about their habits and would do anything to free themselves and their loved ones from the demons that control them. They reach out for help and suffer humiliation when they cannot stop what they are doing, or they anguish silently, unable to control their cravings as they slowly destroy all that they cherish.

Over many years of working with addicts, I have learned the power of compulsive cravings and the good intentions of most who are trapped within them. I have watched, often helplessly, as people swore to stay away from their addictions and could not. But I have also seen many people triumph and go on to help others.

If your relationships have been stolen by your addictions, you must let go of self-castigation or shame to reach for the help that is readily available. The solution is to take responsibility for those you have hurt and do what you can to heal them. You must reach into the deepest part of yourself to find the physical, emotional, and spiritual emptiness that has made you vulnerable to a world that will never take you home. If addictions become your most consistent companion, every partner you love will eventually become angry at your weakness or a hapless rescuer who can never succeed.

THE SEVEN STEPS TO RECOVERY

If you are an addictive relationship saboteur, your partners have always been the third point in a triangle with you and your addiction. Addictions are powerful competitors and most often win, leaving your partners helpless in their wake. When you are able to live your life free of addictive escapes, you will be able to fully enjoy the intimacy that an exclusive partnership provides.

Step One: Observing Your Addictive Behavior Without Judgment

Most addicts begin each new addictive cycle with the absolute intent to give up their compulsions, only to fall prey to them again. They live with shame and humiliation every time that cycle repeats.

To begin your process of recovery, you must stop the internal voices that irrationally reaffirm your attempts and punish your failures. You must also rid yourself of all excuses, explanations, defenses, and promises you have used to gain access to your damaged relationships. As you do the following exercises, try to remain objective and not slip into self-hate or self-justification.

EXERCISE: Your Inner Dialogue

Using your journal, write down two internal monologues. The first will be your promise monologue, and the second will be your rationalization monologue. Here's an example of a promise monologue:

10:00 a.m.: No more alcohol. That party last night did it. I don't even remember how I got home, but my car isn't here, so my girlfriend must have dropped me off. I feel lousy. I can't remember what happened after I threw up in their bathroom. I hate myself when I act like an idiot. I wonder who I offended this time. This behavior is ruining my life. Time to really get serious about quitting. I'll call my buddy today and get to a meeting. I'll call my doctor and get a physical. I'll get over to the gym and start a decent detox. I can do this. This drug doesn't own me. I just need to get a little sleep.

2:00 p.m.: Better get that presentation for work done first. And I need some decent food in the house. The damn phone's been ringing off the hook. I know it's my girlfriend, ready to chew me out again. The pressure is getting to me. I can't possibly get to a meeting this afternoon, but I will tomorrow, first thing. I could sure use a drink, but I know it's the wrong thing to do. Maybe if I just watch the game, I'll settle down.

5:00 p.m.: I'm not getting anything done anyway. The day's pretty much gone. I better call my girlfriend back, or she'll be impossible to deal with. I don't need any lectures. I feel worse than I did this morning. Better eat something.

Here's an example of a rationalization monologue, which, like this one, typically follows a promise monologue:

6:00 p.m.: I'm really shaky, and my stomach hurts. What was I thinking, to just quit cold turkey? I could probably have a seizure or something. I need to have a beer, just to calm down. I can easily stop at one, because I'm not at a party and my friends aren't there to tempt me. It'll help me relax, and I can get that presentation down. I'll get to that meeting in the morning, and I'll get some support. That's a better way to start this deal.

6:30 p.m.: I feel much better. A little alcohol is a great thing. I can get some work done. I'll call my girlfriend to come help me. She's great at the details.

8:00 p.m.: Lousy fight. I told her to get off my back. So, I had a few more beers. What's so wrong with that? I wasn't obnoxious or passing out. She has no right to tell me what to do. Maybe I drink because of her. If I got out of the relationship, I'd probably be okay. This day is over. I'll just have one more beer and get to bed. I can deal with this in the morning. I have the rest of my life to quit drinking.

If this addict and his girlfriend get into a fight over his using alcohol, she will most probably argue from the what-you-promised monologue and he from the I-couldn't-because rationalization monologue. If this addict can get his two internal monologues to forge into an external one with his partner, he will succeed in turning her from a supportive friend into the nagging enemy from whom he can justify escaping into his addictive behavior.

When you are rationalizing your addictive behavior, do you make your inside processes into outside battles with your partner? If you do, you are behaving in a classically addictive pattern.

In arguments with your partner, you may be relieving your own conscience by making your partner assume a certain role. Until your partner leaves the relationship or refuses to play the game, you will be doomed to continue this ineffective pattern.

Step Two: Finding the Taproots of Your Addictive Behavior

Your addictive behavior is not an innate response to stress. You may have been born with susceptibilities to pressure, an inadequate production of pleasure chemicals in your brain, obsessive-compulsive personality characteristics, or a love of hedonistic experiences. Any of these tendencies can make you more vulnerable to addictive programming at any time in your life.

But the learning of addictive patterns usually originates in childhood and is often handed down from generation to generation. You will rarely find an addict without practicing ancestors. The earlier those patterns were modeled for you, the more likely you will have internalized them as automatic responses. The following exercises will help you identify how you were taught your addictive pattern.

EXERCISE: Who Were Your Addictive Role Models?

It takes two people to form the addictive three-way triangle between the addict, his or her partner, and the addiction itself. So you will need to recall two role models from your childhood. The first will be someone who modeled addictive behavior. The other will be the addict's partner.

In your journal, write the name of your addict role model, that person's relationship to you, and his or her type of addiction. Then write the name of the addict's partner, that person's relationship to you, and his or her behavioral response to the addict. List the positive and negative characteristics of each person. You may find that your addict role model was someone you loved and admired, someone you disliked and were frightened of, or some combination of both. You will see how this person holds the power to control the household by reducing anyone around to helpless adapters. Here's an example:

Addict role model: mother

Addiction: clothes shopping

Characteristics: beautiful, classy, self-centered, unavailable, sneaky, private, volatile, sexy, social

Addict's partner: father

Response behavior: helpless martyr

Characteristics: hardworking, resentful, martyred, powerless, kind, frustrated, worried, easily shut down

After you have completed your descriptions of addictive role models in your life, you'll be ready to move on to the next exercise.

EXERCISE: Observing the Interaction

Recall a repeated argument between your two role models. Try to remember when the argument was likely to occur, what was said, and what resulted. Were there usually other people present? If you can recall actual dialogues, all the better. Here's an example, using the sample role models from the previous exercise.

> *The arguments between my mother and father always happened when he returned from work to find that she was still out shopping. My older sisters were usually upstairs talking to their friends when these arguments happened, and I was the only one who heard them. Mom would come in late, looking beautiful and flushed, with several packages in her arms. My dad would be at his desk doing paperwork. She would put the packages down by the door and come in and give him a long, seductive kiss. He would not respond. Then the argument would begin.*

Mom: What's the matter? Aren't you glad to see me?

Dad: How much did you spend?

Mom: Honey, don't be mad at me. Everything was on sale. I bought stuff for the girls and for you, too. It's not that much.

Dad: No one in this house needs any more clothes. Especially you. How much did you spend?

Mom: You always ruin my happiness. You're so cheap.

Dad: I can't support your habit.

Mom: Don't you want to see me looking beautiful?

Dad: Not from my casket.

Mom: You just don't care.

Dad: Forget it.

Now, describe the feelings you had as you watched the argument take place, such as in the following example:

I felt sick inside whenever they fought. My mother had four closets full of clothes, and most of them still had the price tags on them. I knew my father was right, but I wanted to be as beautiful as my mother. I didn't understand why my father just didn't stop her from spending so much money. He always got angry, but he never did anything about it. He would just complain like that, and they wouldn't speak for several days.

After you finish writing, ask yourself if you recognize a pattern you may be repeating in your adult relationships.

You can do this exercise with several different pairs of role models, current or past, and with different addictions. Be aware that Internet addictions to pornography, video games, and online shopping have become prevalent during the last decade. They aren't as obvious as drug and alcohol compulsions, but their effect on relationships can be just as harmful.

Steps Three and Four: Identifying What Triggers Your Addictive Behavior and Examining When You Are Most Susceptible

The events that activate your addictive behavior are ever present when your cravings are just under the surface. How susceptible you are to them can vary from week to week and hour to hour. If you are committed to changing your behavior, the following questions will help you evaluate both your triggers and your current susceptibility:

1. What makes you more likely to follow your addictive pattern?

2. How long have you been involved in this pattern?

3. What prices have you paid for being addicted?

4. In what ways does your present relationship evoke any similar childhood interactions?

5. What alternatives have you tried to redirect your addictive behavior?

6. How clear are you about predicting when you'll use again?

7. Do you excuse or rationalize your addictive behavior?

8. Do your partners, family, colleagues, or friends support or sabotage your desire to change?

9. How vulnerable are you right now to being seduced back into your addictive behavior?

10. How ready are you to leave your addictions behind?

EXERCISE: Assessing Your Susceptibility

Using your journal, answer each of the preceding questions. Your answers will help you evaluate how susceptible you are to letting your addiction control your life. Here are some sample answers:

1. "I am a very anxious person. Marijuana has always calmed me down. I really liked being high at first. Now I'm using it way too much, and probably would have a hard time living without it. I still like being loaded, but I can see that my life isn't working."

2. "I've been smoking grass since I was thirteen. In the beginning, it was just for fun. I'm thirty-eight now and I get stoned every day."

3. "I know I'm way off my career path. I have friends who smoke and are okay. For me, I think, it's wrecked my relationships and my health."

4. "My mom and dad were both heavy drinkers. I hated how they smelled and how they acted. My partner is an alcoholic, but I'm crazy about her sexually, so I keep making excuses to stay. She encourages me to smoke pot, so it's easy to keep breaking my promises to quit. I keep rationalizing that pot is better than alcohol. I've never been able to do anything in moderation, just like my parents. Why didn't I get it that I'd do the same thing with pot?"

5. "When I've been working out regularly, I don't smoke. That's mostly in the summer, when I'm on the beach. The winters are harder. I start to get a little depressed and anxious. I think that's when I'm more susceptible to using again."

6. "I always pretend I'm never going to use again. I don't like to predict it."

7. "I've rationalized my addiction my whole life. I want to stop."

8. "Most of my friends party, but they don't overdo it like I do. They'd really help me if I ever asked them to."

9. "When I'm in a great relationship or busy doing the things I love, I don't smoke very much and I don't even miss it. I'm feeling down right now because my partner just dumped me and my new promotion didn't come through. This would be a time when I'd probably go back to using."

10. "I've never been more ready to stop using."

From this exercise, you can see how a number of factors can band together to strengthen or weaken your vulnerability to your addictive behavior. Increasing your strengths and minimizing your vulnerabilities will help you let go of your self-destructive behavior.

Briefly answer these same questions several times a week until you are able to evaluate yourself quickly and accurately. You'll need to know how you are at all times if you're going to resist temptation and be ready to choose your alternative vision.

Step Five: Learning to Live Your Life Without Addiction

Addictions are like backup lovers when you want out of the relationship responsibilities you're facing. You must stop using your partner or other people as an excuse for remaining an addict. Your goal is to see challenges as opportunities; doing this will strengthen your resistance to your addictive behavior.

You'll need to recommit to practicing self-responsibility every day of your life until it becomes automatic. The next two exercises can help.

EXERCISE: Transforming Excuses into Commitments

Try to recall every excuse, rationalization, or defense you have used to support your reasons for your addictive behavior. The more examples you can recall, the more effective this exercise will be. Try to come up with at least ten. Under each of these pro-addiction statements, write a statement of commitment that invalidates the former. It will help if you exaggerate the point. Here's an example of what an Internet addict might say:

Excuse: I spend several hours on the Internet every day because it helps me relax.

Commitment: Relaxing isn't the real issue. I'm avoiding my responsibilities and wasting time. I know it bothers my partner, and I know it's not good for me, but I can't seem to stop.

Excuse: I am learning so much about the world, and it helps me be a better conversationalist to my partner.

Commitment: I surf the Web continually. Most of it is unimportant, and I don't even remember it. I rarely share any of it with my partner. And I know he would rather make love or do something fun together. I lose track of time and don't seem to care about anything else.

Excuse: I'm sharpening my skills when I play computer games. It makes me think more clearly in the outside world.

Commitment: Boy, that's a lot of B.S. I'm so dopey when I come off those compelling games, I can't think at all. And they keep coming. When I finish one, I'm just as addicted to the next one. Sometimes, I get so little sleep, I can't put two sentences together the next day.

The person in this example may be in a relationship that has ceased to bring novelty or satisfaction. She could be avoiding intimacy or is bored, depressed, or anxious. It's possible that she is not addressing some underlying needs and that addictive behaviors have become a more exciting alternative.

As you try to eliminate your own rationalizations for what you are doing, you'll be able to get closer to what you really need or are avoiding, and see how your addictions are substituting for those needs.

After you complete the exercise, can you see more clearly what you are avoiding and why you are using addictive escapes instead?

EXERCISE: Planning for Alternative Behaviors

Imagine a distressing situation where you would normally cope by choosing addictive behavior. Write about this situation in a series of six statements:

1. Describe the situation and say what distresses you.

2. Express what you want or need to feel better or to help resolve your problem.

3. Write about the addictive escape you normally would use while facing this kind of dilemma.

4. Express how you would feel after choosing this escape.

5. Describe a behavior that you believe would work as an alternative to your addiction.

6. Say how you would feel after making the decision to stay addiction free.

Here's an example from a woman who uses cocaine:

1. "I'm exhausted, and my boyfriend wants me to come over tonight to help him clean his house before the party."

2. "I really need some nurturing and sleep. I wish he'd think about my needs and not always his own."

3. "He'll be disappointed and angry if I don't show up. I could do a line and get some quick energy."

4. "I'd feel high and energized tonight, give him what he wants, stay up all night, have sex, and feel crappy and resentful the next day."

5. "I could tell him what I need and risk that he'll be negative. Then I could take a warm bath and get some sleep."

6. "I'd feel deprived of my fun escape solution, be scared that he wouldn't love me as much, and feel great about taking care of myself."

Next list your fears about giving up your addictive behavior and the risks and benefits of choosing an alternative. The woman in the previous example might write the following:

Fears: "He will leave the relationship because I don't have the energy to do what he wants."

Risks: "I can only keep up with his demands if I keep using."

Benefits: "I will be physically and mentally healthier if I stop using drugs."

Changing addictive behaviors is a long-term, difficult journey. You don't want to make promises to yourself that you aren't ready to keep. When you look at your current level of susceptibility, do the benefits outweigh the risks for you? If you feel doubtful, what would you have to change in your life to make that possible?

The woman in the previous example might answer those questions this way:

I am very susceptible to using right now. I'm too afraid that my boyfriend will leave, and I don't have a strong enough support network to fall back on, because I've devoted so much of myself to him and I'm addicted to my drug. I need to get some help to get clean first and to reconnect with other people I care about. I want to get away from this destructive relationship, and I will.

Leaving addictions behind can only happen when where you're going has a greater magnetic pull than where you've been. Being aware of the price of staying addicted and the promise of recovery will help you stay on track.

Step Six: Finding Witnesses and Support for Conquering Your Addictions

You are less likely to conquer your addictions without outside help. The internal dialogues that have both chastised and excused your behaviors, the relationships you have sabotaged, the harm you have done to your body and spirit, and the well-worn path of temptation over personal integrity are potent forces that can pull you away from your commitment. To counter these forces, you need to reach out to straight-talking, objective witnesses who understand your process.

Using your current partner is always a risk. Anyone who has been with you for a while is either benefiting from your sabotaging behavior or too fed up to tolerate your promises. Your partner might make the critical error of taking on the responsibility of watching over your recovery. Nothing sets off addicts more than being pseudo-parented when they need to take responsibility for themselves. Recovery from addiction is about keeping promises to yourself, not about performing for someone else.

You're much better off reaching out to groups of people who not only have traveled your path but also have triumphed over their own temptations. Alcoholics Anonymous has offshoot groups for many of the more common addictions, and the Internet can afford you virtual cotravelers in every addictive category there is. If you are willing to create your own blog, that effort will give you the added benefit of demonstrating success to those who may still be trapped.

An in-house addiction recovery program or an outpatient program can give you a structured setting that includes detoxing and extensive education about addiction. These programs are less available for the subset of addictions that are now just coming to light, but you could start one in your neighborhood and be guaranteed instant members.

Step Seven: Staying Focused

This is always the hardest step for an addict. Most addicts do very well at the beginning of a commitment but later have difficulty avoiding familiar escape patterns.

If you are serious about changing your life, you must understand that the temptation to backslide will be with you for a long time, perhaps always.

But you will become stronger as time goes by and you continue practicing your alternative behaviors. You need to practice self-forgiveness without slipping into self-indulgence, which is not an easy differentiation for an addict.

To help you stay focused, keep your journal up to date, rely on your cheering squad, diligently practice your alternative behaviors, and regularly monitor your susceptibility. You can also make one more commitment that could make the difference.

EXERCISE: Choosing Consequences Up Front

Imagine that you have a sacred place where you kneel each day to recommit to being the person you want to be. This altar is the repository of the values, beliefs, and behaviors that define who you are at your best. From outside that place of personal light comes the pull of temptation that will ask you to forsake your sacred beliefs. Addictive cravings reassure you that it will be only a temporary transgression. Even though you know this to be a lie, and have had multiple experiences that have proven that, you think maybe you won't have to pay the price this time.

In your journal, try to recall the times in your life when you have fallen prey to that seduction and then had to face the consequences you had hoped to evade. Here's an example:

> I knew I'd had too much to drink, but it was early in the evening and my apartment was only two blocks away. The cops don't canvass my neighborhood this early on a weeknight, and I thought I could drive really slowly so I could fly under the radar. I know that drinking and driving are off my list, but this felt like an okay exception. I was sure it would be okay. Calling my girlfriend to bail me out of jail was humiliating enough, but knowing that I drove my new BMW into a parked car is more than I can bear.

After you've come up with your own examples, you'll see how fruitless it is to believe in addictive exceptions to your sacred commitments.

You will need to reaffirm your commitments at your own altar place each day by following these six rules:

- Whatever you decide to do, your intentions and actions must be integrated.

- You will have zero tolerance for breaking any of your own commitments once you have chosen them.

- If you decide to break your promise, you will accept the consequences up front as part of the whole package.

- You will not allow yourself to excuse or defend your transgressions.

- You will not lie to yourself or another if you break your word.

- If you choose to break a promise, you will go back to your altar place and recommit.

You can leave your addictive behavior behind and choose and win a better life. You cannot imagine the joy of freedom that will result. It takes patience, support, and conviction, but you can do it if you don't give up.

10

Martyrdom: "Maybe It'll Be My Turn Someday"

Saints or scapegoats, suffering victims or benevolent self-sacrificers, relationship-sabotaging martyrs can be the most giving and the most frustrating of partners. At times they may seem completely content in their selfless generosity, without resentment or unfulfilled wants. Then, often unpredictably, their emotions cross some invisible line, and they feel hurt and unappreciated, delivering emotional credit-card debts to their unsuspecting partners.

Whether they are aware of it or not, sabotaging martyrs give to get, hoping their unasked for generosity will create obligatory reciprocity in their partners. Classic examples are the enmeshed mother, the long-suffering partner of an addict, or the ever-present friend who tries to be irreplaceable. Martyrs seldom allow their partners to do anything for them but keep a quiet record of their one-sided sacrifices as leverage for another time.

HIDDEN AGENDAS

If you have played the part of a martyr, you may rationalize that you are just blessed with more to give and are proud of your ability to sacrifice without needing something in return.

But somewhere in the back of your mind, you may know that your selfless behavior has limits. Your basic nature may be to give, and you intend to do that without expectation. But you're only human. Everyone needs appreciation and reciprocal nurturing sometime.

Perhaps you've been taught that it's wrong to ask for what hasn't already been offered. Maybe, deep inside, you don't feel worthy of being cared for. To ask for reciprocity may feel inappropriate.

If you keep giving without recognition or appreciation, however, you will build up resentment. At some point, both you and your partner will feel the shift. If your partner ignores your covert messages, you'll find yourself tracking his or her selfishness, and your initial feelings of generosity will be replaced with self-righteous bitterness. Though you may not speak your feelings aloud, you may be thinking thoughts like these:

"You need to keep track of what I selflessly do for you and feel damn lucky I'm in your life."

"You could never pay me back for all that I do for you, so you'd better not hurt me or let me down when I need you."

"I hope you realize how much I've sacrificed for you and what it's cost me."

RECIPROCAL ATTRACTION

If you have been a martyr in your relationships, you are likely to have attracted either exploiters or indentured dependents. Exploiters are people who don't suffer remorse when they get more than they give. They can easily take without feeling any obligation to return the favor. Their credo is: "If it's offered, I assume I can take it. I don't owe them for that."

Indentured dependents are people who need what you are offering but don't have the emotional or physical resources to reciprocate. They rationalize that you really don't want anything in return or that maybe they will be able to pay it back someday. As their debt to you grows, so does their dependency. When they realize they have incurred a debt they can never repay, they will blame you for causing them to feel obligated, and use their anger as justification for leaving the relationship. Their credo is: "I never asked for all this devotion. It was all your idea, and now you feel ripped off. I told you I can't give like you do, and you said it was okay. I feel betrayed."

If you have been a martyred saboteur in your adult relationships, your partners will have had only these options: to take advantage of you, to try to outdo you, or to get out before they incur a debt they cannot pay.

WHERE DID YOU LEARN YOUR MARTYRDOM?

Marytrdom is a learned behavior. Perhaps you watched one of your parents selflessly sacrificing or were taught that people who give up their own needs are more valuable. Maybe you were rewarded as a child for giving away the things you cared about. Or you may have been the victim of abuse and continue to give too much in the hope that it might buy off anticipated pain.

Your painful experiences may have left you not trusting that others will ever care for you. Giving what you wish you could have had is a way around feeling your own needs. As long as you are on the giving side, you won't have to face feeling unworthy of receiving.

Whatever happened in your life that trained you to overly give, you have the power to change the way you act. You may then discover a treasure you haven't known before, to be loved for who you are rather than for what you give.

THE SEVEN STEPS TO RECOVERY

Whatever your reasons for becoming a martyr, you can change your sabotaging behavior. If you can make yourself the recipient of your own generosity, you will find your transition remarkably achievable.

Step One: Observing Your Martyred Behavior Without Judgment

Like other saboteurs, you will have internal judgments when you observe your behaviors, but your judgments won't necessarily be negative. If you were taught that givers are admired and receivers are less worthy, you will have internal voices that reward you every time you give. Be careful not to let that positive validation divert your commitment to change.

Giving too much is harmful not only to your partners but also to you. As you become aware of that reality, your inner voices may become more negative. If they do, let the self-judgment go. You won't be able to learn as well if you feel bad about who you've been. The goal of the following exercise is to recall how your martyred giving has negatively affected your relationships. Just observe what you do and the results.

EXERCISE: Understanding When Giving Is Manipulative

In your journal, recall three relationships where you feel you gave much more than you received. At the top of each journal entry, write the name of the person and his or her relationship to you. Underneath, describe what you repeatedly did for that person that he or she did not ask you to do. Then write down your feelings about what you did, how you wanted and expected your partner to feel, your partner's actual response, and your reaction. Here's an example.

Jeremy: boyfriend

Action: I went to his house when he was at work, and did all of his laundry, unasked.

Feelings: Felt happy that I could help him when he's so busy. I thought he would appreciate me for it, and I felt good that I had made his life easier. I knew that he liked to take care of himself and didn't usually want his privacy invaded, but I decided that the benefits far outweighed the negatives. I was sure he would see how good my intentions were and how much I cared for him. I felt important and confident.

Expectations: I wanted him to feel loved and taken care of, and to feel good about what I'd done. I guess I also wanted him to appreciate my gift and how thoughtful I am.

Partner's response: He was irritated with me and wouldn't talk to me afterward. He told me he preferred taking care of himself. Later, he gave me a perfunctory apology and said he knew I was only trying to make him happy, but he stayed withdrawn the rest of the week.

Reactions: I felt hurt and totally misunderstood. It isn't the first time he hasn't appreciated what I do for him, but he usually gets over it and realizes it's because I love him. Then he sometimes tells me later that it was okay. I

146

wonder when he'll see how good I am for him and commit to a long-term relationship.

After completing the exercise, consider what have you learned about yourself:

1. You gave your partner something because you wanted to do it, but he or she did not request it.

2. You gave because it gave you pleasure, not necessarily because your partner would feel pleased.

3. You did have expectations, though you may have not wanted to acknowledge them at the time.

4. Your partner disliked what you did and resented that you wanted him or her to be appreciative.

5. You wanted to feel important and needed, but instead you felt unappreciated and hurt, and have felt that way many times before.

You have put money in a psychological bank with a hole in the bottom. The more you do that in your relationships, the more the difference will be between what you think you are owed and what your partner feels obligated to return. After enough similar interactions, your self-appointed goodness will eventually give way to feelings of resentment and victimization, and your partner will feel that you manipulated him or her into owing you something in return.

Step Two: Finding the Taproots of Your Martyred Behavior

This step asks you to look at the significant people in your childhood who measured their self-worth by how much they gave. They modeled for you that giving is a more valuable behavior than taking. What they didn't tell you is that they took pride in their higher status and kept that imbalance in order to feel good about themselves. They also neglected to point out that some of the people they were devoted to became self-involved and spoiled.

In the next exercise, you're going to recall the people in your life who modeled self-denial as a way to hold on to their saint-victim status and convinced people that their selflessness was honorable.

EXERCISE: Identifying the Martyrs from Your Past

Recall the personalities of all the martyrs you have known. Start with the martyr who affected you the most as a child. Describe this person's behaviors and how you responded to each of them. Notice that the problem is usually not the behavior so much as how it affected the relationship. Here's an example:

1. Dad's behavior: Never spent money on himself.

   Your response: "I was glad to have the things I needed, but I felt guilty."

2. Dad's behavior: Always did things for others.

   Your response: "I was proud of him but saw he couldn't say no."

3. Dad's behavior: Never said one mean thing to my mom.

   Your response: "I felt like a bad person when I got angry at my mom."

4. Dad's behavior: Always stopped what he was doing if I needed him.

   Your response: "I worried that I was always asking too much."

5. Dad's behavior: Didn't ask anything from anyone.

   Your response: "He made me feel like I had nothing to offer."

6. Dad's behavior: Suffered his problems in silence.

   Response: "I felt like I should never complain."

7. Dad's behavior: Hurt if he was ever criticized.

   Your response: "I learned to be careful not to notice his faults."

8. Dad's behavior: Always felt righteous.

   Your response: "I could not challenge him."

As you do this exercise, do you have a better sense of what your partner must feel when you constantly give up your own desires to make him or her happy?

Now think of another martyr from your past. Did these different martyrs in your life share some personality characteristics? Continue doing the exercise until you feel you can identify the martyred behaviors you have internalized.

Once you expose and understand the origins of your behavior, you can learn the skills to leave it behind.

Step Three: Identifying What Triggers Your Martyred Behavior

When martyrs try to stop giving, they often feel anxious. Feelings of anxiety, fear, guilt, and inadequacy can drive people to keep giving in their adult relationships even when it's unwarranted. To help you look for those triggers in your current life, you'll need to uncover your underlying negative apprehensions.

EXERCISE: What Fears Underlie Your Overgiving?

Using your journal, complete the following statements:

"If I don't give advice to my partner when I think he or she needs it, I'm afraid that..."

"If I'm not always available to my partner, I worry that..."

"If I don't accept everything my partner says and does, I fear that..."

"If my partner needs stroking and I don't do it, I fear that..."

"I'm afraid if I say no, my partner will..."

"If I show anger or disappointment, I'm afraid my partner will..."

"If I ask too much, I think that my partner will..."

"If I don't give in to a dispute, my partner will…"

"If I find fault or complain, I think my partner will…"

"If I ask for what I need, I fear that…"

Your responses will help you identify your current triggers. For instance, if you completed the first statement with "…my partner will make a mistake and it will be my fault," then your trigger is the fear that you will let someone down. If you completed the second sentence with something like "…my partner will find someone else," then your trigger might be worrying that you will lose your partner if he or she finds someone who is more responsive.

As you do this exercise, you may recall some childhood responses that are similar to what you are feeling now. Write those down as well.

This exercise helps you recognize the deeper feelings beneath your giving role. Many of those fears would not materialize were you to change your actions. Bringing them out in the open most always results in a better resolution.

Step Four: Examining When You Are Most Susceptible to Playing the Martyr

Staying a martyred saboteur requires a partner who will play the other half. Your partner will likely:

- Be attracted to your availability and agreeability.

- Enjoy having his or her needs anticipated and met.

- Give you positive reinforcement at the beginning of the relationship.

- Not fight you when you refuse attempts at reciprocity.

- Believe that you are happy doing what you're doing.

The moment you enter this martyr-user relationship, you'll be in danger of your reserves depleting over time. Please don't expect your partner to resist the free nourishment when it's offered so willingly.

As your supplies deplete, and you have revved up your emotional and physical engines as far as you can, your needs will eventually emerge. When they do, you won't be able to keep giving as freely as before. If your partner is in the relationship because of your selfless devotion, he or she probably won't know how to take care of you. The resulting immobilization is the most common reason that martyr relationships dissolve.

RECOGNIZING WHEN YOU'RE IN A DOWNWARD SPIRAL

Most relationship-sabotaging martyrs focus more on their partner's reactions than on their own reserves. As a result, martyrs often cannot recognize their own self-destruction until their relationships are in trouble. They may be physically exhausted, emotionally drained, mentally confused, sexually flat, or spiritually empty, and still fail to consider giving up trying to please.

You may not be in touch with your own feelings, but you can recognize when you're in a downward spiral by your partner's reactions. At this point, an exploitive partner might say something like:

"You never do anything right. What's the matter with you?"

"Don't make any plans without consulting me first."

"You need to work out more."

"Why don't you take some cooking lessons? This stuff is uninteresting."

"You're getting lazy in bed."

Alternatively, a dependent partner might say something along these lines:

"I really liked it when you made breakfast more often."

"You've been gone a lot lately."

"I could use more back rubs if you can make some time for me."

"Don't you think you're doing a little too much for other people?"

"You're not as nice as you used to be."

If your relationship has reached this point, then you have placed yourself at the mercy of your own self-denial and have hurt yourself in the process. The good news is you can avoid such painful criticisms by learning to be more in touch with your feelings so that you recognize earlier on when you are beginning to feel exploited. At that point you can challenge the relationship or, if necessary, leave it with your self-esteem more intact.

Step Five: Learning to Balance Giving and Receiving

Letting go of your giving-receiving imbalance might bring on strong feelings of insecurity, anxiety, and loss of identity. You've gotten a lot of strokes from giving in the past, and separating what's desirable from what's destructive can be difficult. Trusting that any partner worth having really wants to take care of you can be a considerable leap for a self-sacrificing person.

You may currently be in a relationship with someone you have trained to take more than give. When you start asking for more, your partner might invalidate your requests and make you doubt your right to ask. If that happens, you will need to choose your new behavior over the relationship. Though that choice may be difficult, the alternative would be worse.

If you are single, you are probably giving too much in your relationships with others. You can practice balancing giving and receiving until you are with a new partner.

As you search for a better balance, you may fear you will take too much. You are in little danger of doing that because of your deeply ingrained habit of doing the opposite.

EXERCISE: Searching for Healthy Self-Preserving Behavior

The goal of this exercise is to help you develop a healthy self-preserving side. Rate how true each of the following statements is for you on a scale of 1 to 5, where 1 = never, 2 = sometimes, 3 = often, 4 = mostly, and 5 = always.

1. You feel comfortable when your partner remembers what's important to you.

2. You can say no when your partner wants you to do something that hurts you.

3. When your partner challenges your decisions, you don't give in if you don't want to.

4. You can ask for what you want even when your partner has to sacrifice for it.

5. You make sure you're okay before you do something for your partner.

6. You can handle being rejected if your partner is unhappy with your actions.

7. You don't back down if you strongly believe in something, even if your partner objects.

8. You can express it when you don't like something about your partner's behavior.

9. You feel comfortable in the way you take care of yourself in relationships.

Now add up your score. As a martyr saboteur, you will probably score under 15. You're looking to develop a score of more than 30 to be able to balance your desire to give with your ability to equally receive.

For each of the above statements that you gave a rating of 3 or less, vow that you will work on risking more self-preserving behavior. An exploitive partner may not stick around, but a better one will welcome your changes.

Step Six: Finding Witnesses and Support for Seeking Balance

If you have been a martyr:

- You've had difficulty asking for what you want and taking help when you do.

- Your nobility has been formed by denial of your needs.

- Your sense of self may depend on your enduring hardship when you focus on the needs of your partners.

- You value your capacity to sacrifice to make your lover happy.

- You may not trust anyone to help you become more self-preserving while holding on to the positives of the way you have lived and loved.

Those beliefs and behaviors will make it hard for you to reach out now, but finding healthy people who can model reciprocal behavior is crucial to your recovery. Interestingly enough, former caring partners who have loved your indulgence but couldn't pay the price may be good mirrors for you now. If they have remained your friends, they can give you helpful feedback by recalling the interactions that eventually pushed them away. You can ask them what they did value about your behavior and what they would have wanted you to do instead.

It's probably not a good idea to talk to other martyrs about trying to change. They will be too caught up in their own fears. They may try to encourage your martyrdom by telling you how wonderful you are, or if they're still blaming their partners for their own problems, they will be unable to help you take responsibility for your behavior.

If you have good friends who have watched from the sidelines and truly want to encourage your new commitments, you can ask them to do the exercise that you did in step five. They need to score high for you to trust that they practice self-preserving behavior in their own relationships.

Step Seven: Staying Focused

Staying focused will be your hardest challenge. Your current partner may not want to give up those generous parts of you, even though he or she may feel obligated by the imbalances you've created. Others who count on you to always be available and never say no may feel slighted by your new resolve. If you're still in touch with the people you learned your martyrdom from, they may see you as defecting to the other side, choosing to be selfish and unreliable. You may even like yourself less at first, because you're so certain that giving without receiving is nobler.

It may be difficult for you to imagine being loved and respected if you don't give too much. Having lived your life so long as a martyr, you may fear that saying no will cost you the caring you depend on. Controlling others by guilt and obligation may never have been your intent, but now it may be all you trust. Your biggest barrier will be your fear of letting go before seeing that your new way of being is better.

EXERCISE: Seeing the Positives in Self-Serving Behavior

Hopefully this last exercise will help you stay on track and will be fun as well. Pick three people you have known in your life who were totally comfortable in using other people to meet their own needs. You have probably felt disdainful of these kinds of people and have, too often, chosen them as partners, but they will be great mirrors now. Make a list of some of the ways they exploit their partners and how you feel toward them when they do. Here are some examples:

Sam's behavior: He has no trouble asking for, or demanding, the things he wants.

Your feelings: I think he's a selfish jerk.

Sam's behavior: He uses whatever means he has to get what he goes after.

Your feelings: I can't believe how entitled he feels.

Sam's behavior: He never feels bad when other people sacrifice for him.

Your feelings: I don't think he has any conscience at all.

Sam's behavior: He expects other people to set the boundaries, or else he takes what he wants.

Your feelings: How selfish. He just takes advantage of good people who can't say no.

After you have made your lists, go back and find something admirable to say about the people you've chosen. You may have to stretch beyond your negative judgments, but it's very important to do this. For Sam above, you might write, "I'm amazed at his confidence. He's not at all worried that his partner will leave him if he says what he wants."

As you do this exercise, you will begin to see your biases against self-serving behavior. That realization is crucial if you are to stay focused on your goal.

There are positive benefits to self-sacrifice but only if the giver doesn't expect automatic reciprocity. There are also positive benefits to self-serving behavior. People who are comfortable with expressing their needs don't accrue resentment or bitterness. Your commitment to finding the right balance between giving and receiving will allow you to leave your martyrdom behind.

11

Defensiveness: "It's Not My Fault!"

Defensiveness is a natural response to a perceived attack. Most everyone will respond similarly when they feel their self-esteem, value, or truth is on the line. Those fight-flight-freeze responses are built into the human psyche and can turn lovers into enemies.

In a healthy relationship, partners can share constructive criticism, debate fragile issues, and search for mutually acceptable compromises. If either partner begins to see any challenge, mild or intense, as an attack, defensiveness has replaced the search for understanding. Defensive saboteurs cannot accept defeat. If challenged, they will vehemently argue with their partners until they back down or disconnect.

SEVEN COMMON DEFENSIVE MANEUVERS

Defensive relationship saboteurs commonly use one or more of the following seven defensive maneuvers when they feel threatened. Do you typically react in any of these ways?

Justifying your behavior by making excuses: When your partner finds fault with you, your response is to try to excuse what you've done by justifying the circumstances.

Arguing that your partner doesn't have the facts right: When confronted with something you've done that has upset your partner, you often argue that he or she doesn't "get it."

Telling your partner that he or she is crazy: When your partner complains about something that he or she doesn't like, you are likely to retort that he or she is irrational and unjustified.

Withdrawing to win by disconnecting: If you can't get your partner to take back his or her critical comments, you withdraw and refuse to listen anymore.

Coming up with an exception to the accusation that invalidates it: If your partner uses the word "never" or "ever," you will come up with exceptions to invalidate the accusation.

Exaggerating the accusation to make it look foolish: If you can't get your partner to see things your way, you exaggerate his or her negative comments to make the accusation ridiculous.

Reversing the blame: You are likely to respond to a criticism by flipping the blame and accusing your partner of the same behavior or worse.

If you are absolutely honest with yourself and realize that you often respond to challenges in these ways, take heart. It may be embarrassing to admit that you are a defensive saboteur, but your behavior will be relatively easy to heal.

Most defensive people don't even realize that they have been reacting the way they do. They don't see how consistently and urgently they respond to any criticism or how they cling to their point of view. They do know that they end up in continuous arguments with their partners, struggling to hold on to their righteousness.

WHAT IS LIKELY TO SET OFF YOUR DEFENSIVE SABOTAGE?

Your reaction to a verbal challenge may vary dramatically in different situations and with different people. Depending on how comfortable you are with your partner, a chance remark could bring on painful disappointment or only mild distress. If you're feeling particularly sensitive, you might experience you partner's attacks as mean, even when your partner may only be teasing and intends no harm.

If you perceive an attack as hurtful, you're going to defend yourself more passionately. You'll also be more reactive if you have a history of being criticized in the same general area by other significant people. Likewise, if you have always been a sensitive person, you may be offended by a minor slight that others would ignore.

Timing is essential too. If your partner were to imply that you seemed a little pudgy, you might be more distressed if you were on your way to an important social event than if you had already started your diet. Or if you're overloaded by other demands just when your partner finds fault with something you've done, you may take offense when otherwise you might not.

A strong sense of self-esteem can be an effective protection. But, even if you are basically resilient, you can still take something harder if it strikes a painful chord.

Finally, you may take criticism more readily from some people than from others. You probably take criticism from a partner more to heart than criticism from someone who is less significant in your life, especially if your partner reminds you of someone from your childhood who challenged you in the same way.

WHEN DEFENSIVENESS BECOMES RELATIONSHIP SABOTAGE

Continuous defensiveness tells your partner that he or she can never find fault, ask for a new behavior, or question something you've said or done without your becoming defensive. You're asking to be seen as acceptable at all times, no matter what you think, do, or say.

Unfortunately, defensive people rarely walk away from arguments feeling triumphant. They know that their continual battles with their partner are not good for the relationship, and leave both partners feeling exhausted. They feel just as bad when they lose face as they do when they push their partners into self-doubt. It's a lose-lose situation. Whatever clarity two people might have found in their differences becomes lost in these reactive responses.

THE SEVEN STEPS TO RECOVERY

Learning to give up defensiveness requires a new way of responding to challenges. But before you can change your repetitive defensive behavior, you must recognize when you're being defensive, where you learned it, and what triggers you.

Step One: Observing Your Defensive Behavior Without Judgment

As soon as you think your partner has made a challenging remark, your defensive reactions will begin. You'll use one or more of the seven most common defensive maneuvers to invalidate your partner's views. That counter-challenge will set off a counter-defense, where your partner will attempt to invalidate your defensiveness. Your voices will rise; you'll intensify your responses and continue arguing until someone gets too tired to go on. That battle is over, but so is any current intimate connection.

Couples seeing videos of themselves fighting this way usually feel embarrassed and try to blame each other for starting the battle. The assignment of responsibility becomes a contest no one wants to win.

In the following exercise, you will examine how your defensive fights evolve. As you do, don't try to identify the responsible party. Your task here is simply to observe with compassion and understanding.

EXERCISE: Identifying Your Defensive Reactions

Recall an often-repeated argument between your partner and you where you felt challenged and responded defensively. In your journal, write down the specific defensive dialogue according to your best recollection. Now look at the seven most common defensive maneuvers described earlier in the chapter. Identify your own defensive response in the dialogue and think about what resulted. Note that your partner will counter-defend, but don't pay attention to his or her responses. This is about you.

In the following example, the accuser is male and the defender is female, but it could just as easily have been presented in any gender combination:

Him: I think you had too much to drink at the party tonight. You were slurring your words.

Her: How could you possibly have been paying attention to me? You were drunk, yourself.

Him: I'm not trying to make you feel bad. I just thought you'd want to know.

Her: Why don't you just call me an alcoholic, if you're so worried? Anything else you think is wrong with me?

Him: Look, I just thought I'd mention it. No big deal.

Her: Well, while we're on criticizing, what about that woman you were talking to? Looked a little cozy to me.

Him: That was my boss's secretary. What the hell are you talking about?

Her: You always try to minimize my concerns. Why can't you ever listen to me?

Him: You're nuts. I'm going to bed.

You can see what the woman's defensive response is, reversing the blame by accusing her partner of doing the same thing or worse. She is trying to change his mind by getting him to doubt his position. If she succeeds, she will invalidate any truth in his accusation and avoid responsibility for her own actions.

As you do this exercise, remember that any response to a challenge or criticism that seeks to invalidate the accusation and transfer responsibility to your partner is a defense. The goal in this exercise is not to find fault with defending but to see how that attempt to transfer responsibility occurs.

EXERCISE: Taking Responsibility

Taking responsibility for your own actions is the first step in changing your defensive behavior. That doesn't mean automatically accepting something that isn't true, but it means looking at your own behavior rather than your partner's.

Using the same scenario you recalled in the previous exercise, look for what may be true about what your partner is saying. Write a short paragraph about the truth in the accusation and what happened when you got defensive with your partner. Here's what the woman in the previous exercise might write:

I did have a little too much to drink, and I was embarrassed when my partner confronted me with it. I defended by counterattacking. When he tried to back down a little, I couldn't let go. I exaggerated what he said as if that were what he actually meant, so he'd feel guilty. Then I changed the subject and attacked him for something he did. He got offended and started to back away. I tried to hold on to the conversation, but he wouldn't talk. I felt lonely and scared.

Now that you know what you felt inside and where you may have agreed with your partner's challenges, do not judge yourself. You won't be able to understand your defensiveness if you allow it to emerge here.

The hardest part may be to recognize what you've been doing to sabotage your relationships. Once you do, you may find it relatively easy to learn how to transform your defensiveness into receptivity.

Step Two: Finding the Taproots of Your Defensive Behavior

Defensiveness is a learned response. Children who witness conflicts between their parents or other significant people see how effectively defensive people can avoid responsibility for their actions. If you grew up in a family where defensiveness was a constant way of interacting, you will well remember the growing tension within those battles and the lack of resolution that resulted.

Some families spar in mutual defensiveness as a way to toughen each other. They attack and counterattack as if in combat. The winners take all, and the losers back down. The stakes are high, and no one is allowed to challenge the process.

Other families attack in an indirect way. They expect their members to quietly attend to what they've done wrong and keep their defenses internal. They may wrap a challenging remark in a pseudo-compliment, sarcasm, or an exaggerated negative reaction.

Hierarchical families, where power is given to one or a few, may allow the most powerful member to be exempt from counterattack. That person can insult, complain, or challenge any other member of the family but may not be challenged in return. Children, or other subordinates who are raised in these families, keep their defenses unspoken, waiting for their chance to take on the power role in their adult relationships.

EXERCISE: Your Earliest Memory of Defensive Interactions

To understand where your defensive responses began, you must go back to your earliest memories of watching others in defensive battles or of reacting defensively yourself. In your journal, re-create one of these memories. As you write, answer the following questions: Who started the interaction? What was the relationship between the two people involved? Did it seem as if you had experienced this before? What did both people feel? Did the situation escalate? Who won and who backed down? Did other people get into the act? Was the result predictable? How did the people relate to each other when it was over? Here's an example:

> *I was about ten years old. My dad was watching TV. My mom came in after dinner and tried to talk to him. He wanted to keep watching his show. She stood up and put her hands on her hips and told him he was boring. She was angry and, I think, frustrated. He reacted sarcastically and told her he couldn't remember the last time she said anything interesting. She told him he should go find a woman who would hold his attention. He told her she was being stupid and overreacting. They were yelling. My mom started to cry and left the room. My dad looked guilty, but he didn't do anything about it. They didn't talk for a week. There was a lot of tension in the house. I'd watched this interaction many times before. It made me sick.*

When you have completed your own scenario, can you identify which of the seven common defensive maneuvers were used in this interaction? Which of these do you employ most often in your adult relationships? Can you sense the underlying fears of being invalidated that both people feel when a defensive battle is going on?

EXERCISE: Identifying the Origins of Your Defensive Reactions

In your journal, describe a situation from childhood where you were particularly susceptible to something that happened that set off a defensive reaction. Write down any details you can remember and the defenses you used. Write down what defensive maneuvers you may still use in your adult relationships. Here's an example:

> I am very reactive to being told I can't do something. I was sickly as a teenager and my mother was overprotective. She wouldn't let me go out with my friends and made me go to bed when I wasn't tired. I argued with her about her being too controlling, but she wouldn't listen. If my partner tries to tell me I can't do something, I get rebellious and do whatever I want. The defenses I use are withdrawal and invalidating my partner's arguments. My level of reactivity is very high. I almost can't hear what my partner is trying to tell me for fear my confidence will be erased again.

As you come up with more memories from childhood, you will be able to more clearly see what patterns you have unconsciously brought from the past into the present.

Step Three: Identifying What Triggers Your Defensive Behavior

Most triggers have childhood roots. Families have their specific issues that often are brought up repeatedly in defensive arguments. You have internalized those issues whether you participated in those family arguments or just observed them. In situations that feel similar to those you experienced as a child, the same issues may come up for you.

EXERCISE: Finding Possible Trigger Areas

Many people are sensitive about specific topics, such as their political beliefs, religious beliefs, families, pets, physical appearance, sexuality, friends, intellect, emotional responses, need for space, special kind of music, need to work out, desire for affection, fears, work, love of travel, or desire for special foods. Note in your journal if any of these topics or others are particularly sensitive for you, both past and present. Then rate how important each of these topics is to you on a scale of 1 to 5, where 1 = not very important, 2 = somewhat important, 3 = often important, 4 = very important, and 5 = can't do without it.

The more attached you are to a belief, possession, or desire, the more likely you are to be defensive if your current partner teases you about it. A rating of 3 or higher means this is a sensitive subject for you. A rating of 1 or 2 means that you will be more open to hearing your partner's point of view.

Telling your partner where your defensive buttons are will tell you if he or she is willing to accommodate them. Partners who focus in on your sensitive areas and use them against you are looking for a fight.

Step Four: Examining When You Are Most Susceptible to Defensiveness

Once you have identified your defensive buttons, you'll need to see how your current relationship activates them. Remember, when you are stressed in other areas of your life, tired, ill, or pushed in too many directions, you will react more strongly even if the triggers are mild. Earlier, this chapter discussed several factors that can significantly affect how susceptible you may be to sabotaging your current relationship. In this next exercise, you can evaluate what your own vulnerabilities may be.

EXERCISE: When Are You Most Susceptible?

In your journal, write a short paragraph that answers each of the following questions: How secure do you feel in your current relationship? Are there any particular areas that you feel more sensitive to? What is your history of being criticized in that area? What do you believe your partner's motivation is for challenging you? How resilient is your inborn sensitivity? Would this be a good time for you to be challenged? What's your level of psychological and physical health right now? How important is this relationship to you? Here's an example:

> *I'm very secure with my current partner. We are excited about a future together. But I am worried that he and I aren't on the same page when it comes to our religious beliefs, and about how that will affect raising children. He keeps trying to tell me that my trust in God is irrational and keeps me dependent and unable to trust myself. I was raised in a very religious family and was constantly teased about our rituals by outsiders. I'm usually a pretty resilient person, but I'm going through some tough times right now and questioning myself about my beliefs. I've lost three great friends in the last year to cancer, and I wonder why they were taken so young. I really love my boyfriend and I want this relationship to work, but we argue about this all the time. I just can't seem to stop.*

Ask yourself where your own current vulnerabilities lie and if those areas are where you are the most defensive.

Step Five: Learning How to Leave Defensiveness Behind

There are some clear steps you can learn that will allow you to hold on to your own point of view without having to invalidate your partner. You may want to practice these steps in imagined interactions before trying them while under attack. When your partner challenges your opinions, behaviors, or feelings, follow these rules:

Start with getting more information. Ask for examples and what your partner would have preferred. Ask how your transgression bothered your partner and why. Get your partner to talk about the situation and how important it is. The best way to neutralize an attack is to understand it better without needing to invalidate the complaint. It's only your partner's point of view, not necessarily the only valid one. You can always challenge it after you've listened deeply if you still feel that you need to.

Feed the information back without altering it. Tell your partner what you heard and ask him or her if what you heard is correct. Make sure your voice is not sarcastic and that you're not trying to make your partner feel wrong about what he or she said. Keep checking until your partner says you're on target.

Ask if your partner is ready to hear your side of the story. The best way to make sure your partner is ready to hear you is to ask. After you've listened to your partner, he or she may be more willing to hear your side.

Tell your partner how you feel. This is a crucial time not to try to convince your partner that your way is more correct. Instead, give more information about why you chose to do what you did. Sharing your feelings and your view of the situation is the right thing to do.

Ask for your partner's feedback. You want to make sure your partner heard you correctly.

Say what you are willing or unwilling to do to change the situation. Share your intentions and reasons with caring and compassion, whether or not you agree with your partner.

Unless your partner's motive is to rile up the relationship or use your defensiveness as a way to leave, he or she will respond positively to this process. If your partner insists on holding on to his or her negative feelings, you may have to temporarily disconnect and try again when your partner is more receptive.

Step Six: Finding Witnesses and Support for Giving Up Defensiveness

This step is the easiest one to take, but it must be done in a relationship with someone you trust, who won't take advantage of your vulnerability.

EXERCISE: Challenging Your Defensiveness

Pick someone you know well, who understands and respects your strongest attachments and why you feel so upset when they are threatened. It can be a friend, family member, partner, or therapist.

Choose three important trigger areas, such as things you strongly believe in. Make certain they are intense attachments, those that would be difficult to let go. Now have your friend dramatically exaggerate an attack on that sensitive area. Using the methods described in step five, practice your nondefensive responses. If you are too uncomfortable, change to a topic that's less painful until you are more comfortable. When you become more confident, ask the person to step up the attack and invalidation again. See if you can stay nondefensive and clear. If you can bring some humor into the interaction, it will help.

Practicing your nondefensive responses with a supportive friend will make it easier to choose those responses when you are triggered in a love relationship. As you become more comfortable with your new capacity to listen before you react, you will find that many of your defensive reactions not only were unnecessary but also created differences that never had to be.

Step Seven: Staying Focused

Your last step is to keep yourself from slipping back into the old ways. Hopefully, you're feeling much better about your capability to change your defensive behavior and your success has become its own reward.

One of the best ways to remind you of your commitments is to watch interactions in movies and on TV when people begin to attack and defend. Defensiveness is one of the most common relationship-sabotaging behaviors. You won't have to listen for long before you hear the exaggerated reactions and the escalating mutual threats of people in defensive battles. Pay attention to when there might have been nondefensive interventions that would have uncovered more information and perhaps turned the argumentative battle into a search for mutual truth. Similarly, remind yourself to watch for defensive behavior in your own relationship and to replace it with the more productive behavior you have learned.

12

Trust Breakers:
"I Never Really Agreed to That"

If there's one sabotaging behavior that surpasses all the rest in its ability to damage relationships, it is the breaking of trust. The loss of credibility that follows erodes partnerships at their very core.

Trust is based on three sacred agreements:

1. Both partners will uphold mutually chosen values, ethics, desires, and behaviors.

2. Neither partner will allow exceptions to those agreements without prior negotiation.

3. If either partner breaks the agreements, that person must acknowledge it, accept responsibility, and express authentic remorse. If both partners agree, they can renegotiate their agreement and put better safeguards in place. Otherwise, trust cannot be restored.

Some trust-breaking behaviors are more likely to destroy relationships than others: infidelity, core addictions, the unilateral squandering of mutual resources, breaking the law, or withholding crucial information. The disrespect, disdain, heartbreak, and destruction that follow such betrayals is often irreparable.

Trust-breaking relationship saboteurs may be more subtle in what they do, so subtle that their negative behaviors often go unnoticed in the early stages of relationships. When compensated by positives, these behaviors often present no serious threat, but as time passes, they can become irritating enough to cause a relationship to flounder and even fail.

Chronic promise breakers are usually expert excuse makers and superb strategists after the fact. Their stated good intentions, repeated offenses, and ingenious escapes from accountability can leave their partners doubting their own sanity.

Ultimately, it's not one acute event but the accumulation of disappointments that eventually becomes unbearable to their partners. No matter how willing partners are to forgive or how attached they may be to their lovers, they will eventually stop believing anything they are told. Whatever intimacy existed gives way when the heart cannot trust and the mind can no longer believe.

BROKEN PROMISES AND NEGATIVE SURPRISES

Trust breakers disenchant by repeatedly promising that an event will occur and consistently failing to come through. They may know that they will be unable to deliver but avoid revealing it to their partners because they aren't willing to pay the price for being honest. They are experts at giving misinformation, procrastinating, spinning a tale to give it a false twist, or pretending not to have said or done something that actually occurred.

If the trust-breaking partner appears truly remorseful, compassionate, and committed to changing his or her future behavior, the betrayed partner will usually forgive the transgressions, at least for a while. Looking forward to a better outcome, the betrayed partner wants to believe that the broken promises will stop.

But if the behavior continues, those ever-mounting excuses become hollow and harder to believe. Eventually the trust breaker's partner must choose between believing in the improbable or giving up hope that trust is possible. A famous example is Charlie Brown's ongoing belief that Lucy won't suddenly pull away the football just before he tries to kick it the next time.

ARE YOU GUILTY OF REPEATED TRUST BREAKING?

Let's assume that you mean well and haven't wanted to hurt your partners, but you still are guilty of repeatedly breaking their trust. Let's even give you the benefit of the doubt; you really believe that your inability to keep your word is mostly beyond your control. There are just too many unexpected and unpredictable catastrophes.

But your partners aren't listening anymore. They've gone from trust to suspicion to disbelief and have finally left you because they have concluded that you are not the person you promised you would be, but the one you've turned out to be.

Now you realize that you need to change your trust-breaking behavior, but you don't know how. You've spent too much energy creating rationalizations and aren't sure anymore what you can and cannot deliver.

THE SEVEN STEPS TO RECOVERY

Chronic trust breakers lack credibility not only with their partners but ultimately with themselves as well. The great news is that, when given the opportunity and skills to change, they are among the most highly motivated of all the relationship saboteurs.

Step One: Observing Your Trust-Breaking Behavior Without Judgment

This step is always the most difficult for well-intentioned trust breakers. You may find yourself quickly moving from objective observation to your rationalizations. It can be difficult to simply take responsibility for what you've done without trying to justify it, considering the list of legitimate excuses you've created over the years.

The purpose of the next exercise is to help you look more honestly at your behavior. That may feel embarrassing, but you won't be able to change what you cannot see. As you observe, you may hear the hurt and angry voices of past partners in your mind. They are the repositories of your negative self-judgments. Try to put them aside for now.

EXERCISE: Comparing Your Intentions with the Results

In your journal, write down at least ten promises you've made in a significant relationship that you couldn't keep. Those you've repeated many times will have the greatest impact.

Put each promise in quotes, as if you were speaking to your partner in the present. Then, write what you felt inside but were afraid to tell your partner. Write down how your partner responded when you were unable to keep your promise. Remember to stay objective and nonjudgmental. Here are some examples:

Promise: "I'll be back in an hour."

Truth: *There's no way I can get back by then, but I don't think he'll wait for me if I say I'll be there later. I think I can patch things up when I get there.*

What happened: When I finally arrived, my partner wouldn't answer the door at first. I had to beg him to forgive me again. He said it would be the last time.

Promise: "That's really all the money I owe, sweetheart."

Truth: *I'll get that loan paid off before she knows about it. Won't be a problem.*

What happened: She found out about the money when the overdue notice came to the apartment. Now she doesn't believe anything I say.

Promise: "I told you I would do that in a week? You must have heard me wrong. I never said that."

Truth: *I do sort of remember making a promise, but I can't let her know she's right. She would never forgive me. Besides, maybe she did hear me wrong.*

What happened: I finally confessed because I couldn't stand making her crazy. She told me she could have forgiven me if I'd only been straight from the beginning, but now she wonders whether she should stay with me or not.

After recalling your own examples, are you better able to separate your intentions from what you actually do?

When you make a promise in the future, ask yourself in advance how likely it is you will be able keep it. If you're with the right partner, your relationship will benefit from sharing any doubts you have up front.

Step Two: Finding the Taproots of Your Trust-Breaking Behavior

When, where, and whom to trust is one of the first things children learn. If this important foundation is shaken by broken promises, the ability to trust or to be trusted will become an issue in later relationships. To find the origins of your own behavior, you'll need to look at the people who first broke your trust and then made excuses for their behavior. That combination of broken trust and excuse-making probably resembles what you've been doing with your partner.

EXERCISE: Connecting the Present to the Past

Recall a significant person in your childhood who repeatedly or intermittingly made promises to you that he or she didn't keep. In your journal, write about an important event where this person broke a promise. Then describe the two- or three-way dialogue that occurred afterward. Here's an example:

> *I remember playing soccer. I was nine years old and was picked to be the goalie. My dad traveled a lot in his business, so he couldn't be a coach, but he promised me he'd make it to my games. Every week, he wouldn't be able to make it, but he'd tell me all the important reasons why he was detained. All the other dads were there, and some of them traveled too. I tried to believe him, but after a while, it was hard to.*

Me: Dad, you promised to come to the game on Saturday.

Dad: I know, sport, and I truly meant to. It's these darn meetings. I just never know when they're going to happen. You know I'm always there in spirit, and I will make it next week. I told everyone on my team they'd have to cover for me this time. I won't disappoint you again.

Me: But, Dad, you said that last week.

Dad: Was that last week? Are you sure I didn't make it last week?

Me: No, Dad. You haven't been to a game this season. And I'm the goalie.

Mom: Now, honey, leave your poor dad alone. He tries the best he can to do everything that's expected of him. He can't always come through on everything he promises.

Me: I'm not talking about everything. I'm just talking about my game.

Mom: You're not being understanding or respectful of your dad's hard work. He'll do it when he can. You know he wants to be there.

Dad: Your mom's right.

Me: I guess so.

After re-creating your own dialogue, can you see where the combination of broken promises, excuses, and rationalizations originated? In your journal, answer the following questions to help find the origins of your current trust-breaking behavior:

- Do you treat your adult partners the way you were treated as a child?

- Do you use the same excuses and rationalizations?

- Do you try to blame your trust-breaking behavior on circumstances out of your control?

- Do you try to blame your partner for expecting too much when you can't deliver?

Step Three: Identifying What Triggers Your Trust-Breaking Behavior

Your childhood disappointments may affect your current relationships in three important ways. Though you may not have intended to betray your partner, you may have done the following:

- Offered things you didn't deliver.

- Promised things you really didn't want to do.

- Run out of time or energy or not set aside the resources you needed when the time came to deliver on what you promised.

Having disappointed your partner as you were once disappointed, you most likely have felt a compelling desire to make things better. That urgency inevitably leads to new promises, equally unlikely to come true, followed by more excuses when they do not.

Your current triggers can be anything that activates those promise-and-fail patterns. Your fear is that saying no to your partner when he or she asks you for something will result in anger, disappointment, or the loss of love. Worried about the consequences, you may put your agreement out of your mind and forget that you made the promise in the first place.

EXERCISE: Taking a Closer Look

Go back to the exercise in step one, where you recalled several promises you made to a partner that you could not keep. Pick one that seems particularly significant. When you take a closer look, can you perceive the honest reaction that you stifled out of fear of loss? Can you imagine what might have happened if you had been totally honest and only promised what you were more certain you could deliver? To imagine a new response, this time expand the exercise. Write down your partner's request, the trigger, what you promised your partner, your actual behavior, your excuse to your partner, what you told yourself, the real reason, and an honest response to the original request. These eight steps are illustrated in the following example of broken trust:

1. Partner's request: "Can you get my prescription today by five o'clock?"

2. Trigger: I felt an obligation to please.

3. Promise: "I'd be happy to do that for you."

4. Behavior: I couldn't get there in time.

5. Excuse to partner: "My watch stopped, and by the time I realized what time it was, I couldn't get my friends to leave the party and get me to the pharmacy on time. It wasn't my fault."

6. Real reason: I can't ever keep track of time when I'm having a good time, but I couldn't say no because he hardly ever asks for anything and I felt too selfish.

7. Expanded reason: My partner asked me to pick up a prescription for him by five o'clock on Saturday because he had a chance to play golf and couldn't get back in time. I had planned a day at the beach without any time limits. I felt a little resentful but didn't want to disappoint my partner, and I've forgotten to do things I promised in the past because I often run out of time. I agreed to pick up the prescription for him and had all the intentions in the world to keep my word. In the back of my mind, I knew the girls I was going with are notorious for running late, but I thought that this time they wouldn't keep me. I felt a slight uneasiness inside, but I ignored it. When it came time to leave, my friends were at the bar and told me they weren't ready to go. I panicked and began to formulate an excuse. By the time my partner came home, I felt guilty and tried to find a way to make it up to him. He'd heard too many of my excuses and wasn't interested in being compensated. I felt terrible.

8. Same request but honest response to his request: "I feel really conflicted. I want to be there for you, but I'm not good at planning time when I'm having fun. There'll be five other girls with me, and I'm not driving. They like to party, and I'm sure they'll be lit by the late afternoon. I don't want to worry about not getting back in time or disappointing you. Can it wait until tomorrow, or can we find someone else to pick up the prescription?"

Go through your own dialogue and complete the same eight steps. Can you see how much you put yourself and your partner through by not being willing to accurately predict your own behavior? You may fear that your partner will be angry or disappointed with you if you're honest up front. This fear blots out past memories of how much more angry your partner has felt after you've broken your promise and keeps you from planning better when the next opportunity arises.

Step Four: Examining When You Are Most Susceptible to Breaking Trust

Your triggers are anything that causes you to agree to something you don't want to do, can't accomplish, don't know how to do, or haven't the resources to make happen. To determine your susceptibility to a current trigger, you can ask yourself the following questions:

- How many times have you broken that promise before?

- How many times have you felt guilty and remorseful about hurting your partner?

- How many excuses have you used for your behavior in the past?

- How many similar interactions can you remember from your childhood?

- How many times has your partner gotten upset when you broke his or her trust?

- How many times have your partners threatened to leave you because of your promise breaking?

- How many times have you avoided being honest about your true intentions?

Broken promises and excuses lead to more broken promises and excuses. The greater the number, the more likely you are to be susceptible to your triggers.

EXERCISE: Evaluating Your Current Susceptibility

Recall a recent event where you made a promise you didn't keep and risked your partner's trust. Describe the situation and what your partner asked of you. Then, answer each of the seven questions listed earlier in this step, rating your responses on a scale of 1 to 5, where 1 = not a lot, 2 = some, 3 = more than you'd like, 4 = quite a few, and 5 = way too many. This will give you a susceptibility score. The higher your score, the more susceptibility you'll have to the current trigger and the more likely you'll get yourself in trouble. Here's an example:

My partner has just asked me if I would please try to lose a few pounds before our vacation to Hawaii in a month. She told me she loves me, but I'd be more attractive to her if I were a little slimmer.

1. I've probably made that promise every year for the last ten years. The chances of actually doing something about it in two weeks when I'm working overtime is next to zero. Susceptibility score = 5.

2. I've felt horrendously guilty more times than I can count. Susceptibility score = 5.

3. Too many. Susceptibility score = 5.

4. My mom promised my dad every month she would lose weight and never did. He never stopped asking and she never stopped feeling inadequate. Susceptibility score = 5.

5. She is wonderful about it. I think she really doesn't expect me to, and she tells me all the time how attracted she is to me. I think she feels my guilt and keeps giving me an opportunity to change it. Susceptibility score = 3.

6. I feel incredibly secure. I wonder why I just don't face my limitations and stop going along with this charade or actually lose weight and stop disappointing myself. Susceptibility score = 0.

7. I don't really know how many times I've avoided being honest about it. I don't want to be like my mom, so I've been pretending to be different. It's my own reactions I'm uncomfortable with. Susceptibility score = 2.

Total score = 20.

After creating your own example, add up your score. A score between 0 and 15 means you are not that reactive to this trigger. A score between 16 and 24 puts you on alert to buy some time before you respond to make sure you can predict your behavior accurately. A score of 25 to 35 means you are likely to give in to your fears and make promises you can't keep.

If you have a high score for certain triggers, you may be so insecure about the loss of someone's love that you are immobilized. But if you continue to let yourself be controlled by those fears, you will ultimately lose the relationship you are trying so hard to keep. A better alternative would be to challenge those fears up front.

Step Five: Learning How to Give Up Your Trust-Breaking Behavior

To build back trust with your current partner or ensure that you will be trusted in a new relationship, you must make the following commitment: before you make a promise to your partner to be somewhere, do something, respond in some way, or change your thinking, first check in with yourself to see if you can honestly keep that promise. The following exercise will help.

EXERCISE: Your No-Flake Policy

The goal of this exercise is to replace trust breaking with credibility. Before you agree to any request, ask yourself how you would answer these questions:

1. Does the request feel legitimate?

2. Do you have the resources at hand to grant what's being asked of you?

3. Do you want to do what has been asked of you? If not, why?

4. What might be likely to keep you from keeping your word?

5. Have you used those excuses before?

6. Do you think your partner can believe in your commitment to change?

7. Could your partner help you to keep your commitment?

8. What childhood trust-breaking memories could affect this particular promise?

179

9. What is your susceptibility level right now?

Practice answering these questions in your journal using sample interactions from the past. When you are comfortable and can answer them rapidly in real time, you will be more likely to respond appropriately to your partner's requests.

As you practice greater honesty, you will begin to feel a sense of lightness as the yoke of guilt around your neck begins to lift. Even if you lose the relationship you're in, you'll never again suffer from the fear of being a trust-breaking fugitive.

Step Six: Finding Witnesses and Support for Being Trustworthy

This is the easiest step for people to take who want to be trusted again. There are probably many people who still care about you despite the times you have let them down. If you are not in a relationship now, you can reach out to some of these people now. They might enjoy helping you practice your new honesty.

EXERCISE: Safe Practicing in Real Time

Choose someone who has experienced your trust-breaking behavior yet still cares enough about you to have stuck around. Tell this person what you have learned and ask for help. If your friend agrees to participate, ask him or her to make up a request that represents other times when you have broken a promise. Pretend that this is a real request. You want the truth, even if it's uncomfortable to hear.

Next, have this person ask you the no-flake questions from the exercise in step five. Answer the questions as honestly as you can. Then discuss whether this person believes that you are telling the truth this time. Try to keep the exercise as loving and nonjudgmental as possible. Afterward, ask this person if his or her feelings about trusting you have changed. Are your own feelings about yourself any different?

You can do this exercise with several different people to practice your new behaviors. The more you come from an authentic place, the more people will be able to trust that you are who you say you are.

Step Seven: Staying Focused

The best way to stay focused on trust building will be to constantly practice. That means saying no when you need to say no and meaning yes when you say yes. It also means keeping appointments on time, keeping your word or renegotiating agreements, and not pretending you didn't make a promise or blaming your own mistakes on others when you slip. For a while, you'll need to keep track of the times you are on target and the times you slip.

EXERCISE: Your Promise Chart

Just before bed each night, write down up to three commitments you made earlier that day. They can be simple ones, like promising yourself that you would call a friend, or more major ones, like doing those fifty abdominal crunches. If you made promises to be met at some specific point in the future, complete this next part of the exercise on the day you agreed to meet those commitments.

After each statement of commitment, rate how well you met it on a scale of 1 to 5, where 1 = totally flaked, 2 = made an effort but didn't succeed, 3 = partially completed it, 4 = mostly completed it, and 5 = actually did it.

Do this exercise regularly, and you'll see improvement over time. You're going to need a lot of encouragement from the friends who have agreed to help you and, most importantly, from yourself. Don't be overly forgiving and don't condemn yourself. Just keep putting out the intention. Eventually you will succeed. As you leave trust breaking behind, you'll receive a bonus: the ability to understand and let go of any residual hurt or anger toward the people who taught you to be this way.

Revisiting the
Seven Steps to Recovery

Relationship sabotage comes in many different forms, but the outcome is always the same: the loss of a once-loving partner who has become emotionally allergic to the saboteur's destructive habits. Most relationship saboteurs are not intentionally destructive. They don't set out to torment their partners or destroy their relationships. In fact, most are heartsick about what they've done. Their repetitive behaviors are all they have ever known, and they often pick partners with sabotaging behaviors of their own.

If you believe you have been a relationship saboteur and are willing to look at your patterns of behavior, your recovery can be rapid and effective. With personal understanding and acceptance, you can replace your sabotaging habits with behavior that will guarantee success.

THE SEVEN STEPS TO RECOVERY REVISITED

The seven steps to recovery and the exercises in this book have addressed the behaviors of the ten most common relationship saboteurs. This chapter will add some exercises with universal application. As you do these exercises, you'll learn more about yourself and how to leave problem behavior behind. Practicing them regularly will integrate your mind and heart in a new way. As you improve your own response strategies, you'll attract partners who are more likely to want the kind of relationship that you want. As you work through the exercises, you may have unexpected thoughts, ideas, or emotions, so continue to keep your journal handy.

Step One: Observing Your Behavior Without Judgment

In this step, your goal is to seek the invisible. You cannot change what you cannot see, and self-criticism is the enemy of awareness. Do everything you can to leave any feelings of failure, self-disdain, or embarrassment behind. This is the time to become an objective reporter on your own behavior. Don't focus on failure or allow negative self-judgment to cloud your observations. Your task is to carefully observe your own behavior and look for patterns as if you were your own objective and compassionate therapist.

EXERCISE: Practicing Objectivity in Symbolic Conflict

Think of a relationship conflict you have experienced repeatedly. Your goal in this exercise is to stand aside and watch yourself and your partner in the conflict as if you were a compassionate and unbiased observer. Imagine that the conflict is happening in the present. Describe it in as much detail as possible. Take your time and recall as many details as you can. Adding dialogue will help it feel more real.

Visualize the interaction as though it were a movie. Answer the following questions. Who are the people involved? Where does the conflict take place? What time of day is it? What were the events leading up to the conflict? What feelings are being expressed and how? What is each person complaining about? What do you think they want of each other? What do they seem to be defending? What are they accusing each other of? What do you believe the outcome will be? Do you think it will be what both partners want it to be? Here's an example:

> I am watching a man and woman in their bedroom. It's late in
> the evening. The woman has been out late for several nights in a
> row, telling her partner she was at work. He seems frightened and
> insecure and keeps asking her questions. She's getting more defensive
> and angry. He wants reassurance, and she keeps telling him he's
> crazy. Each person wants the other to listen and care, but they can't
> hear each other. He feels hurt that she doesn't seem to care about his

insecurity. She feels defensive because he isn't sympathetic about how hard she's been working and how tired she is. Neither one seems able to stop. They aren't going to resolve this, and they'll go to bed angry, which neither of them wants.

As you watched yourself in your own scenario, were you able to stay compassionate and nonjudgmental about your own behavior? How did you feel as you answered the questions? Were you able to see patterns you didn't see before? Do you remember any similar interactions you may have witnessed as a child? How do you feel now, after completing this exercise?

Once you can observe your sabotaging behavior without self-judgment, you can begin to look for its origins. In all likelihood, you originally developed your behavior as a coping response to challenges from your childhood. Frightening or painful experiences can happen at any time in life, but they have the greatest impact when you are young and helpless. Early memories are the most deeply etched in the mind and heart.

Step Two: Finding the Taproots of Your Behavior

As you observe your behavior, you will begin to feel the tug of taproots, those central lifelines that take you back to your formative early experiences. When something in your present life reminds you of a painful episode from the past, you may experience a negative inner dialogue that sounds like something that may have happened long ago. Recognizing your negative inner dialogues and recalling when they first happened are the first steps to changing them.

EXERCISE: Listening to Your Inner Dialogue

Think of a situation in a current relationship where you felt threatened. Listen for the negative internal dialogue that emerged. In your journal, write about the situation and why you felt threatened. Then re-create the dialogue to the best of your recollection. See if you can find the parental voice that invalidates you. An example might be the following threat of being emotionally erased.

*My boyfriend paid attention to everyone else at the dinner table
except me. I felt devalued and insignificant. I tried to get him
to talk to me, but he was too involved with people he obviously
preferred talking to. I wanted to leave the restaurant, but I felt
frozen to my seat and humiliated. The feelings felt strangely familiar.*

This woman realized she was having the following inner dialogue:

Me: I really need attention.

Parental voice: You don't deserve it.

Me: I guess I should be grateful for what I have.

Parental voice: And not complain.

Me: I'm feeling so insignificant and insecure.

Parental voice: That's because you want too much.

To discover where your negative inner dialogues originated, remember a significant adult in your childhood who talked to you and others in this way. Remember an episode where this person was talking to you and recall the dialogue. Be as detailed as you can. Answer the following: Who is speaking? What is this person's tone of voice? What does this person want of you? How do you feel on the receiving end? What are you trying to say back? What do you think is going to happen? What do you want to happen?

Here is an example of a dialogue from one of my patients who was trying to change her need for control and power in her relationships:

*I'm eight years old and I need help with math from my father. He's
watching television, and I'm afraid to approach him. I've been
trying my best to do the problems on my own, but I can't figure out
what to do. No one else is around. I already feel stupid, and I know
my dad doesn't like me to interrupt him.*

Father: What do you want?

Me: I need some help with my homework.

Father: Why can't you do it yourself?

Me: I don't understand it.

Father: You're just lazy.

Me: No, I'm not. I work really hard.

Father: You always have an excuse, don't you?

Me: Never mind. I'll figure it out.

Father: See, I was right. You were just trying to get out of it.

Me: *(Feeling stupid and insecure.)*

My father's tone is impatient and irritated. He doesn't want to be bothered. I feel rejected and unimportant. I want to tell him that I need him, but I know he will yell at me and I'm afraid of his anger. He'll tell me I'm stupid. I wish he wouldn't make me feel so bad. I wish he would say he's sorry for scaring me.

In her adult relationships, the woman experienced again that internalized dialogue and the accompanying feelings. When she became threatened, the dialogue replayed in her head. She couldn't bear feeling stupid, so she played her father's role and made her partners feel stupid instead. Her feelings of inadequacy drove her to be controlling so she could define the rules.

In re-creating your own dialogues, your goal is to understand where your sabotaging behaviors began. The greater the impact of the dialogue, the clearer these patterns will be. As you do this exercise, watch for changes in your breathing, physical posture, or facial expressions. If you are overcome by emotion, stop for a while and rest before you begin again.

By now, you will have identified your specific sabotaging behavior and its origins. The goal of the following exercises is to create new options in your present relationships. Understanding and reframing your early experiences will allow you to change how they affect the present.

EXERCISE: Dialogue of Hope

This exercise is designed to help you replace the punishing, invalidating, or neglecting parent in your head and heart with the parent you wish you'd had. You will compare three dialogues:

1. A dialogue from your childhood. You can use one from the previous exercise or create a new one.

2. The dialogue you wish you'd had instead.

3. A dialogue that hasn't happened yet: the dialogue you would like to happen when you are triggered in the future.

To begin, choose a dialogue that was often repeated, for it will have had a greater impact. Remember where you were when the hurtful childhood interaction occurred, who you were with, and how old you were. Occasionally, your memories may feel too early to be verbalized, in which case you can use simple emotions instead of words to describe what happened.

You'll know if you're on the right track when your body responds emotionally and physically to your memories. You may sense yourself recoiling if the memories are too hurtful, or just feeling sad, angry, confused, or frustrated. Note any differences in your body posturing, such as hanging your head, crossing your arms, or biting your lower lip to hold back tears.

The following is an example of one man's childhood memory:

I am an only child with a depressed and martyred mother. No matter what I do to try to make her feel better, I can't help. I continue to put my own needs aside so that I won't burden her. For all it matters, I might as well not be there, but I feel guilty for not being more adequate. I'm afraid she will die.

Parent: I can't imagine anything in my life ever turning out right.

Child: It'll be okay, Mom. I'll help you. *(Wanting to be good.)*

Parent: There's nothing you can do.

Child: I can, I can. I'll make you some tea. Okay? *(Trying to make a difference.)*

Parent: My stomach is in knots. It won't help.

Child: Should I call your sister to come over? *(Feeling powerless.)*

Parent: No, don't bother anyone. I'll be all right. She never makes it better.

Child: I'll get my homework and do it right near you. *(Fearful of abandonment.)*

Parent: Do whatever you want. It doesn't matter.

Child: *(Guilty, defeated, and invalidated.)*

Here's how the man looking back at this conversation re-created the conversation, becoming the parent he wishes he'd had.

Parent: I can't imagine anything in my life ever turning out right.

Child: It'll be okay, Mom. I'll help you.

Parent: That's so kind of you, sweetheart. I can see how much you want to help.

Child: I'm scared that we won't be okay. *(Safe to show vulnerability.)*

Parent: I'm so sorry to frighten you, baby. Things are just a little hard right now.

Child: Will it turn out all right? *(Searching for security.)*

Parent: We'll make it turn out all right. We're a great team, aren't we?

Child: Should I call Aunt Fran to come and help?

Parent: What a great idea. You're so smart.

Child: *(Feeling reassured, important, and needed.)*

The third step is to create a dialogue of the future, a situation where you express your feelings and your current partner responds in a helpful way. Here's an example of where you might express futility and your partner responds in a way that helps.

You:	This day was a complete disaster. Everything that could go wrong did.
Your partner:	You sound beat. Anything I can do to help?
You:	No one can—wait a minute. Yes, just tell me I'm not crazy and things are going to be okay.
Your partner:	You're not crazy at all. You're just beat. It'll work out eventually. Whatever it is, we'll face it together, remember?
You:	Thanks, babe. I don't want to be like my mother, always drowning in her sorrow. I really appreciate your support.

Now create your own three dialogues. Looking back at your childhood dialogue, ask yourself the following questions: What did you need and what happened instead? What could the adult have done differently to make you feel safe and cared for? Knowing what you know now, could you have done anything that could have changed the situation? Have you unconsciously been repeating the roles from your childhood in your adult relationships? What behaviors in your partner are most likely to activate your triggers? Can you see more clearly where those patterns began?

If you can catch your hurtful childhood patterns as they reoccur in your present relationship, they will be easier to turn around. Being able to see them coming, stop them from happening, and choose a better way to respond will become more automatic with practice.

Step Three: Identifying the Triggers

Once you know the triggers that activate your negative behaviors, you can watch for them in your present relationships. Some triggers may be influenced by genetics or the result of a childhood trauma. Those will always be with you and will be noticeable from the onset of any relationship.

Other triggers may be a learned response to less-damaging childhood interactions.

Whatever their impact, if you can identify these triggers and where they originated, you'll be able to catch yourself before you automatically react to them. You will be able to slow down and give yourself time to choose a different response.

The current triggers in your relationship can include anything that activates an early life experience. You might respond to your partner's facial expression, voice tone, body language, words, emotional state, desires, or challenges. You'll know that an interaction is bringing up a negative childhood experience when your feelings are more intense, powerful, and emotional than usual.

Your goal is to recognize what has triggered you before your emotional reactivity has begun its spiraling cascade. The next exercise will help you learn to slow things down before your emotional responses have gotten out of hand.

EXERCISE: Catching the Triggers in the Present

Choose some experiences in your significant relationships that have repeatedly set off your sabotaging behavior. You'll know they are triggers to the past because some part of you will wonder why you are having such a strong reaction. You may even feel the same age that you were when your painful experiences first began.

When you have written about those experiences in your journal, answer the following questions for each one. What was the trigger? What was the first moment when you realized you were beginning to react? What sabotaging behavior was triggered?

Do not allow yourself to judge your behavior. Self-criticism will inhibit your learning. If you see trigger patterns, write them down in a separate list labeled "triggers." Here are five examples:

- Insecurity trigger: "My partner tells me that our sex isn't as exciting now." Sabotage: "I can't stop questioning whether the relationship is over or not."

- The need-to-control trigger: "My partner doesn't make it a priority to be with me when we have planned time together." Sabotage: "I repeatedly remind him two hours beforehand."

- Fear-of-intimacy trigger: "My partner wants to plan the next two weekends together." Sabotage: "I tell her that I might have other plans but I won't know for a while."

- Needing-to-win trigger: "My partner tries to convince me that going to church would be good for us." Sabotage: "I tell him that I'm a confirmed atheist and I'm extremely well read on the subject, so there's no point in discussing it further."

- Trust-breaking trigger: "My partner reminds me of our anniversary dinner date, and I realize I've made plans to go to a hockey game the same night. I don't want to disappoint her, so I pretend she didn't remind me in enough time. Sabotage: "I often don't make her needs as important as mine, and I don't want her to leave the relationship, so I try to make things her fault so she'll keep trusting me."

Looking back at the episodes that triggered your sabotaging behavior, can you see a point when you could have stopped your reaction? When and how would you have needed to intervene to keep yourself from escalating?

Step Four: Examining When You Are Most Susceptible

Emotional triggers can vary in their intensity and frequency, depending on what else is going on in your life. Anything that increases your stress level or challenges your emotional resiliency can make you more sensitive to triggers. If you can stay in touch with your feelings, you can become more conscious of your triggers and improve your responses.

The next exercise will help. The best time to do this exercise is when you first awaken in the morning. It will only take a few minutes, and if you do it every day, you will eventually be able to automatically anticipate unexpected negative experiences before they take hold.

EXERCISE: When and How Are You Susceptible?

In each of the following dimensions, rate your resiliency on a scale of 1 to 10, where 1 represents the least resilient and most vulnerable you've ever felt and 10 represents the most resilient and strongest you've ever felt.

Physical: Check out your body from head to toe. How do you feel now compared to the best you've ever felt? Are you on any medications that could affect your capacity to rebound? Have you suffered any physical trauma recently, and if so, are you healing? If you're not at your best, what would help you feel that way again?

Emotional: Where are you on the continuum of emotional well-being, from feeling insignificant and uncared for to feeling loved and fulfilled? It's only human to want to matter to significant people who are a part of your life and care about what happens to you. Have you had any recent losses, and if so, are you still grieving? Are you looking forward to the future? How filled up is your emotional tank?

Sexual: Do you feel deprived of physical touch, affection, and fulfillment, or do you feel content with the amount of sexual satisfaction you are experiencing? Are there people in your life whom you can reach out to when you are in need of physical contact? Touch is a critical part of security. If you are touch-hungry, you will be less able to withstand other deprivations.

Mental: Do you feel confused and uncertain or intellectually awake and engaged? Do you have mental outlets that keep you challenged? Are there people in your life who value your mind and want to know what you think?

Spiritual: When times are especially difficult, having faith in something greater than yourself can make the difference between quitting and staying in the game. If you have a deep faith in something greater than yourself, you will be able to rely on it in times of deprivation or discouragement. Do you feel that you have a spiritual belief that fulfills, inspires, or supports you, or do you feel spiritually dry, hopeless, uninspired, or lost?

Add up your points. The higher your score, the better you'll be able to stay centered, even when a significant trigger emerges. A score of 40 or over means you are strong and can probably bounce back quite easily. If your score is between 21 and 39, you are holding your own. If it's under 20, you are very vulnerable and can easily be seduced into old sabotaging behaviors.

Stay in touch with these measures. Your goal is to be able to evaluate yourself accurately at any time. Just being aware will change the way you respond. Knowing what you need is the first step in self-care.

EXERCISE: Forgiving Yourself

Sometimes your old behavior will be triggered without your realizing it, or you may recognize the behavior but be unable to stop your reaction. Do not expect to stay on top of every experience or keep perfect control of your emotions. Be ready to forgive yourself if you become emotionally triggered despite your best efforts.

If you do slip into old behavior, please give yourself the compassion you need. There is no behavior more destructive than beating yourself up for not getting it right every time.

A simple way to practice forgiveness is to imagine that you are someone else you love dearly, such as a treasured friend. Pretend it's that person who has made the mistake and is slipping into negative self-judgment. Your task is to listen and then help that person acknowledge what was done wrong, accept whatever responsibility is appropriate, and recommit to trying again.

Can you see yourself through this projection, needing desperately to own your mistake but not be buried in self-regret? Can you see how important it is to forgive those errors and to focus on the positive strides you are making? Treat yourself with the same kindness you would have given to your treasured friend. Here is an example of a self-forgiveness dialogue:

You: I feel horrible about what I've done. I know better and I've totally screwed up my relationship again.

Listening self: Tell me what happened.

You: I couldn't ask for what I wanted, and I just manipulated the situation so that my partner would feel obligated. When he found out what I'd done, he told me he wouldn't put up with that martyred crap anymore.

Listening self: What triggered the interaction?

You: I was really tired and I wanted him to take care of me. He just wanted sex and didn't seem to care. So I serviced him and then I felt resentful and angry. He tried to take care of me, but I wouldn't let him. He canceled his plans with his friends that night and took me out to dinner instead. Then I was nice again.

Listening self: What did you learn?

You: He said if I'd just told him what I needed, he would have gladly taken care of me. I didn't think anyone would.

Listening self: What will you do next time?

You: I'll try to be straight.

Listening self: You're looking at your own behavior and not blaming him. That's really important. I'm proud of you.

You: Do you think I'm really worth loving if I don't take care of someone else first?

Listening self: Yes.

Practice your own self-forgiveness dialogues. Remember that negative self-judgment is the enemy of progress. With enough practice, eventually you will be able to self-soothe before your susceptibility to triggers gets out of hand.

Step Five: Seeking a New Vision and Finding Alternative Behavior

Your goal is to let go of your sabotaging behavior and practice new behaviors until they become automatic. To do that, you need to know who you've been, whom you want to become, and what you have to do to change.

It will take discipline and patience to deal with the pulls of the past. Familiar patterns can be cruelly seductive. You must make a commitment to yourself, to others, and to what you know is right. The light at the end of the tunnel is an image of what your relationships will be like when you shed your sabotaging behavior.

To further cheer you on, you can create an internal advocate to counter the negative voices that you may carry around inside. The next two exercises will help you do that.

EXERCISE: Remembering Your Positive Role Models

Recall the people you've known in your past whose qualities you admired and respected. These people have helped you before and can inspire you now.

1.   Make a list of anyone significant who, even under stress, modeled healthy, functional behaviors when you were a child.

2.   List the admirable attributes of each of those people.

3.   Write down your relationship with each person and how you felt about each other.

4.   List what you believe you have learned from these people.

5.   Choose the most impressive people and write letters of appreciation to them. Tell them how important they were to you and why. It's not necessary to send the letters, though you can if you like.

6.   Recall any relationship in your own adult life where you have emulated some of the behaviors on this list.

Next is an example:

It was my third-grade teacher. She was widowed with two small children. Her mother suffered from Alzheimer's and lived with her. She taught during the day and tutored in the evening to make ends meet. She smiled all the time. She was smart, kind, never complaining, loving, patient, encouraging. I adored her. She always had time for me. She thought I was funny. She encouraged my mother to give me more encouragement and not so many rules.

From her, I learned to ask questions before I judged someone and to start every assignment with "I know I can do this." I learned that actions are more important than intentions.

I heard she died of breast cancer two years ago, but her son is teaching in the same school she did. I will write a letter to him to tell him how wonderful she was to me. I wrote a silent letter of appreciation to her in my heart.

I probably have only given that kind of unconditional love to my golden retriever, but I'm going to try to do that with my partner more.

The greater the number of positive role models you can recall, the greater effect the combination of their voices will have.

In the next exercise you will combine the positive attributes of these past role models to create an internal champion who will support you whenever you need cheering on.

EXERCISE: Creating Your Personal Advocate

List all the positive characteristics of the people you described in the previous exercise. Include how these people made you feel about yourself. Summarize what you learned from them.

When you are done, use this information to create your personal advocate. You can give this advocate a name and a physical description. Keep this imaginary person in a safe place in your mind to talk to you when you are in distress. If this advocate becomes part of your internal dialogue, you will be better able to resist the temptation to fall back into sabotaging behavior.

Step Six: Finding Witnesses and Support

You're at a critical crossroads. You don't want to go back, you are not willing to stay where you are, and you don't know exactly where you're going. That's when you need a support group of objective, caring people to help you become the person you want to be. Your supporters can be of any age, of either gender, and have any relationship to you, but they must be able to balance honesty with compassion. Ideally, they should know you deeply, understand and agree with your goals, and be available when you need them. They are not your guides, judges, or teachers; they are your witnesses to your own promises to yourself.

If you're lucky, you'll have found a partner who can play this role for you. Stay away from people who feel sorry for you when the going gets tough or make fun of your attempts to change.

Likewise, avoid asking people with their own agendas. Some people may want your friendship and just say whatever you want to hear. They may have their own axes to grind. They may be in the middle of their own problems and want misery for company.

Consider reconnecting with someone who was able to support you in the past and will tell you when you were off-track. If that person is no longer available, try to find someone else who can play that role. Support groups can be found online, in local papers, and in reference books that list them by geographical area. Note that organizations are only as good as their current members. Expect to spend time and energy finding the right one.

Along with the real people you find to help, you can use your internal advocate. Use your dialogues with your advocate for the support you need now. It especially helps if you write down these dialogues in your journal. You can use them for reference to track your progress.

Step Seven: Staying Focused

When you are transforming your life, it's easy to become discouraged whenever you backslide. Remember that no one can stay on track all the time. You'll need to encourage yourself to keep trying.

You'll also need to keep abreast of your progress, which you can do in a number of ways. Take a few moments once a week to answer these questions:

- Are your self-dialogues changing from critical interactions to those of encouragement and support?

- Can you observe your interactions without self-judgment?

- Can you catch your triggers before you are in danger?

- Do you know when your resiliency is down and you are more susceptible to your triggers?

- Are you staying calmer when your sabotaging behaviors are triggered?

- Are you taking a few moments each morning to pay attention to your emotional, physical, mental, sexual, and spiritual needs?

- Can you forgive yourself when you slip?

- Is your relationship with your personal advocate intact?

- Are you reaching out to your support group when you need help?

- Are you keeping up with your journal entries, so you can record your progress?

You must hold on to the belief that you are capable of changing and that you are absolutely worth every moment of time you give to the process. Keeping that faith is crucial to your success.

EXERCISE: Keeping the Faith

Whenever you feel overwhelmed or your efforts seem to be going too slowly, answer these questions:

- Do you forgive yourself when you backslide?

- Do you reassure the child inside yourself that change is possible?

- Do you watch for temptations when you're vulnerable?

- Do you keep your eye on where you are going and what you will become?

- Do you practice your new behaviors regularly?

- Do you recognize your efforts when you succeed?

- Do you hang out with people who are true helpers?

- Do you remember your strengths when you see your weaknesses?

- Do you focus on others who have made it to the other side?

- If each time you ask these questions, your answers are more often yes than no, you are well on your way to leaving your sabotaging behavior behind. Remember, your sabotaging behavior is not all of you. You have had partners who have been attracted to your positive qualities.

The desirable parts of you are still there. With determination and courage, you will leave the toxic behavior behind. You will be honest, accountable, and confident, able to have the successful relationships you have always wanted.

14

Troubleshooting: Questions and Answers

Facing your relationship-sabotaging behaviors is the hardest part of changing, and you've already accomplished it. You've started a transformation that will improve your current relationship or any relationship you have in the future.

As you progressed through the exercises in this book, you may have come upon unexpected barriers or uncovered old emotional traumas. You may wonder if a lot of other people have suffered similar disappointments and frustrations, and been able to overcome their past relationship failures.

Many people have had similar experiences to yours. These are the questions they've most often asked:

- How do I know if it's really my partner who is sabotaging the relationship but blaming it on me?

- Can my relationship work even if I can't eliminate all my sabotaging behavior?

- Are saboteurs attracted to other saboteurs?

- Do committed partners usually help or hinder your efforts to change?

- Can you have more than one sabotaging behavior?

- Could it be possible that my behaviors are really okay, and my partner is just overreacting?

- Can I stay on track if I'm not currently in a relationship?

- How can I keep from regretting the past?

- Are there other sabotaging behaviors I should be aware of?

This chapter will explore the answers to each of these questions.

HOW CAN YOU TELL IF YOUR PARTNER IS THE REAL SABOTEUR?

It takes courage to look at your own sabotaging behavior, and projecting it onto someone else can be much less uncomfortable. If you think your partner is really the saboteur, you could be blaming him or her for your own problem.

On the other hand, your partner could be a saboteur. He or she may be an expert in getting you to feel responsible when something goes wrong, wanting you to feel doubt about your observations.

Or you might both be at fault. Mutually sabotaging relationships are not uncommon. Exploiters and martyrs, addicts and codependents, power-hungry people and those who must obey, accusers and defenders are all easily recognizable duos who practice counter-sabotage on a regular basis.

The good news is that once you are committed to transforming your own sabotaging behavior, you'll be able to differentiate your own patterns from whatever your partner is doing. There's a foolproof way to tell. As you begin to change, sabotaging partners will do everything possible to get in the way. They have benefited in some way from what you've been doing, and can't continue to get what they want if you leave your negative behavior behind. Partners who are getting nothing out of your old patterns will be encouraging and supportive of your new behavior.

When you initially give up your relationship-sabotaging behavior, your partner may mistrust your new commitment. That's only natural. It may take a while before your partner sees your commitments as sincere. Be patient and give your efforts some time. If your progress continues, you'll eventually win over your partner's resistance.

WHAT IF YOU CAN'T ELIMINATE ALL YOUR SABOTAGING BEHAVIOR?

Your sabotaging behavior is only part of who you are. At the beginning of your relationships, your negative behavior may have gone unnoticed or been overshadowed by your positive qualities. Even if this negative behavior has now created an increasingly more difficult situation, your current partner may love you enough to feel that the whole package is still worth it. If you are honest about who you are and sincere about wanting to change, your partner will feel encouraged by your acknowledgment of your sabotaging behavior and your willingness to try put it behind you.

Some sabotaging behaviors are more easily tolerated than others, and partners with complementary behaviors will have an easier time accepting them. Someone who enjoys being quiet, for instance, may be able to tolerate a center-stage person, whereas a more competitive partner may not. A person who has trouble paying attention to details can appreciate some of the qualities of a micromanager as long as both partners can agree on the terms. An insecure person may be a lifetime occupation for a partner who enjoys feeling needed.

Other sabotaging behaviors, like trust breaking or addiction, are much more likely to destroy relationships. Partners of trust breakers or addicts may fuel their own self-destructive behaviors by indulging the sabotaging behavior of their partners. If your sabotaging behavior is innately destructive, you won't create a healthy relationship until you can leave such behavior behind.

There's also the bad-guys-win theory. Some people have so many positive attributes that they can get away with highly sabotaging behaviors. Talent, beauty, wealth, status, and power are big draws. Most people don't have those advantages, but those who do can order from a smorgasbord of willing partners, many of whom will fall by the wayside in time.

While you work on leaving your sabotaging behavior behind, you can offer your partner some time-honored qualities to keep him or her close to you. Honesty, humility, compassion, remorse, and the willingness to be accountable can make a big difference.

ARE SABOTEURS ATTRACTED TO OTHER SABOTEURS?

Saboteurs can be attracted to other saboteurs, especially if they support each other's behaviors. For example, people who use their power over their partners to exploit or harm them are magnets for those who derive their worth by suffering. People who demand attention attract partners who enjoy the role of adoring sycophant. Those who fear intimacy have more latitude to connect and disconnect with partners who are insecure. People who need to win arguments may enjoy the extended banter that occurs with partners who prolong arguments with defensive reactions.

Relationships between intertwined saboteurs usually fall into repeated patterns that preserve the negative behaviors, but maintaining the delicate balance of two compulsive, mutually reactive behaviors can be hard work. If these relationships endure, it's usually because the partners have some strong additional reasons for staying together, like powerful sexual attraction, mutual obligation, or fear of a worse outcome with someone else.

If you are in a mutually sabotaging relationship, you won't be able to change it unless both of you work together. If you are the only one trying to change, your partner will do everything he or she can to seduce you back into the neurotic balance the two of you have maintained in the past. The resulting instability will be chaotic and potentially destructive. Better to clear your own path and go it alone.

WILL A COMMITTED PARTNER HELP OR HINDER YOUR EFFORTS TO CHANGE?

If you have habitually engaged in sabotaging behavior and the relationship is still intact, you can expect to feel tension when you begin to change your patterns. Even if your relationship has always seemed relatively stable, an underlying tension may have been building.

Keep in mind that long-term committed partners probably do have some investment in your sabotaging behavior and may unconsciously or intentionally try to seduce you into familiar patterns. If your partner's provocations start escalating, you might suspect that something else is going on.

If you're in a new relationship, living off the wonder of initial lust and love, your partner is probably ignoring or tolerating your sabotaging behavior. But even if your partner currently finds your other qualities wonderful enough to compensate, the latter will become more frustrating over time. Showing your partner that you are seriously working on improving will go a long way toward keeping the relationship viable.

The hardest time to change your sabotaging behavior is when your relationship is in trouble. If your partner is already emotionally allergic to your actions, he or she may have little interest in supporting your efforts, especially if the future of the relationship is questionable. You're asking someone who is already looking for reasons to be upset to put those feelings aside and support you. In those cases, it's better for you to show how you've changed rather than advertise your intentions.

It's not all up to you. You may have chosen a partner who, for his or her own reasons, is invested in supporting your sabotaging behavior. Perhaps your partner feels obligated to you because you have been willing to forgive something in return. Maybe your partner has tried everything to get you to change and now wants out even though you are getting better. Perhaps you both just need a little more time to adjust to the changes before you decide.

Hopefully, you've been lucky. Your partner is looking to make changes too and is excited by your willingness to start the process. Whatever your situation, you still can keep your own commitment to change. Your goal to transform your sabotaging behaviors must take precedence over saving your relationship.

CAN YOU HAVE MORE THAN ONE SABOTAGING BEHAVIOR?

You can have more than one sabotaging behavior, and so can your partner. If you grew up in a dysfunctional family where the members acted in multiple sabotaging ways, you will have learned all the parts in a sadly destructive play. If you are attracted to partners who symbolize people from your past, the two of you can play all the parts that re-create your childhood interactions.

Remember, you and your partner are individual pieces in the complicated puzzle of your relationship. The interplay between you is another unique piece of its own. Even if you consistently sabotage the relationship, your behavior may activate different responses with one partner than it would with another.

Your partner's negative reactions will likely become more intense over time, and so will yours. If both of you have multiple sabotaging behaviors, the combination can be volatile and it's more likely the relationship will self-destruct before you get a chance to correct the problems.

The one hope of couples with multiple and mutually sabotaging behaviors in a relationship is that the problems show up early. When the relationship is still new, both partners can be highly motivated to change their negative patterns.

IS YOUR PARTNER JUST OVERREACTING?

Be especially careful about asking if the problem is your partner's. It could be a genuinely appropriate inquiry or a self-delusional trap. Being held accountable for sabotaging behavior isn't easy, and you could be blaming your partner when you should be looking at your own behavior. Or you could be with an overreactive partner who exaggerates your triggers and makes your sabotaging behavior more likely to occur.

But, if you focus on your partner's negative behaviors and neglect your own, you might opt out of the relationship instead of seeing how your problems have contributed to the relationship's failure. If that happens, the chances of your sabotaging behavior recurring in a new relationship are high. The best way to deal with your sabotaging behavior is to deal with it directly. Being afraid to face it will only postpone the inevitable.

It's true that the negative things you've done in other relationships may not affect a new partner in exactly the same way. Or you might even pick someone who doesn't initially trigger your sabotaging reactions. Some partners may love you enough to let your behavior slide for quite a while. But, in time, your behavior will reemerge as a problem, and what seemed to be a compatible relationship may not turn out that way.

Please be careful not to fool yourself. If you've been triggered into sabotaging behavior many times in the past, then your partners have not created it but simply activated what was already there. Even if your new partner doesn't provoke any negative reactions, it doesn't mean your problems are resolved. Sabotaging behaviors seem to have a mind of their own. They resurface again, often when the sabotaging partner least expects them to.

CAN YOU STAY ON TRACK IF YOU'RE SINGLE?

If you are not presently with a partner, you can use this time to learn from the past and prepare for the future. Practicing can be less stressful when you are single. You won't have current scenarios to work with, but you will have pressure-free time to plan.

On the other hand, expectations from a current partner can be a good motivator for continued commitment. It's easy to put transformation aside when the work is difficult and the rewards are not yet in sight. To keep yourself on track, you may need to find a stand-in. Getting feedback from friends or a willing support group can help.

If you've remained friends with past lovers, they may be able to provide quality feedback. They will often be your best critics. The fact that you are still close to an old lover serves as testimony to a good relationship that was not completely destroyed when you broke up. If the other person is willing, you could ask him or her to do some of the exercises with you. This can lead to major breakthroughs and expedite your process.

HOW CAN YOU AVOID REGRETTING THE PAST?

A great tombstone would read, "Many mistakes and few regrets." With each error you make, you can burden yourself with unremitting remorse or express gratitude for the lessons it brings. If you have made a painful error with far-reaching consequences, you may need some time to grieve and to heal. That's appropriate if it helps you move on. Remembering the past is necessary, but too heavy a focus on failures will interfere with your motivation to do better.

It also may be hard for a new partner to listen to distressing experiences from your past. Your new partner may think he or she needs to heal your old wounds, or may identify with your past lover and wonder if you will repeat what you've done before. It's not the responsibility of a new love to either judge or reassure you. You will be better off if you integrate your past lessons first and then come into your new relationship ready to put what you've learned into effect.

This is where successful self-forgiveness is a valuable goal. Go back to the forgiveness exercise in chapter 13 and practice it regularly (see step four). You will eventually be able to move on to your future successes.

ARE THERE OTHER SABOTAGING BEHAVIORS?

The ten sabotaging behaviors discussed in this book are the most common, but there are others that may have special significance in your personal relationships. The seven steps to recovery can address them as well. The exercises in chapter 13 can help you transform any sabotaging behavior that may be threatening your relationship. Here are a few other relationship-sabotaging behaviors to look out for.

Passive-aggressiveness: You promise anything to get out of trouble, but find countless ways to keep from delivering.

Undercutting: You take away any joy or sense of accomplishment from your lover by repeatedly stating how he or she could have done better.

Compulsive fighting: You argue every point just because you like being in opposition.

Manipulating: You always have a hidden agenda but won't admit it.

Blackmailing: You use past mistakes as ammunition when you want something.

Procrastinating: You always have an excuse to do things at the last minute or come in after the race is over.

Withdrawing: You quit when you can't win.

Complaining: You would rather express unhappiness about problems than try to resolve them.

Exploding: You threaten extreme behavior if you don't get what you want, or suppress your feelings until you emotionally blow up.

If you have been a relationship saboteur, you now have the skills to positively change your relationships and your life. You can also recognize sabotaging behaviors in potential partners early in the relationship. The best time to face these behaviors is when love is new and motivations are high. Creating a positive relationship in the present can heal past heartaches and give hope for untold future possibilities.

Suggested Reading

Bourne, Edmund J. 2005. *The Anxiety and Phobia Workbook*. 4th ed. Oakland, CA: New Harbinger Publications.

Brown, Nina W. 2008. *Children of the Self-Absorbed: A Grown-Up's Guide to Getting Over Narcissistic Parents*. 2nd ed. Oakland, CA: New Harbinger Publications.

Hendrix, Harville. 2007. *Getting the Love You Want: A Guide for Couples*. Anniversary ed., rev. and updated. New York: Henry Holt and Company.

Kirshenbaum, Mira. 1997. *Too Good to Leave, Too Bad to Stay: A Step-by-Step Guide to Help You Decide Whether to Stay In or Get Out of Your Relationship*. New York: Penguin Group.

McKay, Matthew, Patrick Fanning, and Kim Paleg. 2206. *Couple Skills: Making Your Relationship Work*. 2nd ed. Oakland, CA: New Harbinger Publications.

Miller, Dusty. 2008. *Stop Running from Love: Three Steps to Overcoming Emotional Distancing and Fear of Intimacy*. Oakland, CA: New Harbinger Publications.

Missildine, W. Hugh. 1963. *Your Inner Child of the Past*. New York: Simon and Schuster.

Roth, Kimberlee, and Freda Friedman. 2003. *Surviving a Borderline Parent: How to Heal Your Childhood Wounds and Build Trust, Boundaries, and Self-Esteem*. Oakland, CA: New Harbinger Publications.

Schnarch, David. 1997. *Passionate Marriage: Keeping Love and Intimacy Alive in Committed Relationships.* New York: Henry Holt and Company.

Seligman, Martin. 2007. *The Optimistic Child: A Proven Program to Safeguard Children Against Depression and Build Lifelong Resilience.* Boston: Houghton Mifflin Harcourt.

Spradlin, Scott. 2003. *Don't Let Your Emotions Run Your Life: How Dialectical Behavior Therapy Can Put You in Control.* Oakland, CA: New Harbinger Publications.

Yalom, Irvin. 2000. *Love's Executioner and Other Tales of Psychotherapy.* New York: HarperCollins Publishers.

Randi Gunther, Ph.D., is a clinical psychologist and marriage counselor in Lomita, CA. She has given multiple workshops and lectures, inspiring hundreds of couples to go beyond their limitations to create successful relationships. A practical idealist, she encourages her patients to give up their deadlocked limitations and to create the relationships of their dreams. In more than forty years of practice, she has spent over 90,000 face-to-face hours helping individuals and couples.